D0209542

Beyond Me was so cool to read! It reminded me just how much you can impact someone's life. I loved it! I am truly humbled and honored to be Melinda's friend.

—Sheila E.

Not only was Melinda one of the best contestants to ever grace the *American Idol* stage, she possessed a humility that left many dumbfounded, including Simon Cowell. Because I knew Melinda before either of us were on *American Idol*, I could confidently tell doubters that her kindness and generosity of spirit were true. She is the real deal. And through *Beyond Me* people will now get a chance to understand why.

—Mandisa

I've had the opportunity to work with a lot of great people and I've observed how people react to a "star." It's different with Melinda. Sure, people are "wowed" by her celebrity. But it runs far deeper than that. When people meet Melinda for the first time—they immediately feel connected. It's what made her so popular on *American Idol*. She is genuine and approachable. And she has a down-to-earth, common sense about her that is beyond her years.

I'm privileged to have Melinda as a friend. Her talent is tremendous and her heart is enormous.

—Michael W. Smith

I've been the recipient of Melinda's encouragement. So has my daughter Sarah, after her first public performance. Melinda practices what she preaches. We are all better for her.

—Amy Grant

melinda doolittle

with *New York Times* Bestselling Author Ken Abraham

BEYOND ME

Finding Your Way to Life's Next Level

ZONDERVAN®

A WORTHY BOOK

ZONDERVAN.com/
AUTHORTRACKER
follow your favorite authors

ZONDERVAN

Beyond Me
Copyright © 2010 by Melinda Doolittle
This title is also available as a Zondervan ebook.
Visit www.zondervan.com/ebooks.

This title is also available in a Zondervan audio edition.
Visit www.zondervan.fm.

Requests for information should be addressed to:

Zondervan, *Grand Rapids, Michigan 49530*

Library of Congress Cataloging-in-Publication Data

Doolittle, Melinda, 1977-
Beyond me : finding your way to life's next level / Melinda Doolittle with Ken Abraham.
p. cm.
ISBN 978-0-310-32744-8 (hardcover, jacketed)
1. Doolittle, Melinda, 1977- 2. Christian biography—United States.
3. Singers—United States—Biography. 4. American idol (Television program).
5. Success—Religious aspects—Christianity. I. Abraham, Ken. II. Title.
BR1725.D66A3 2010
277.3'083092—dc22 [B] 2010001911

All Scripture quotations, unless otherwise indicated, are taken from the Holy Bible, *New International Version®, NIV®*. Copyright © 1973, 1978, 1984 by Biblica, Inc.™ Used by permission of Zondervan. All rights reserved worldwide.

Scripture quotations marked AMP are taken from the *Amplified® Bible*, copyright © 1954, 1958, 1962, 1964, 1965, 1987 by The Lockman Foundation. Used by permission. (www.Lockman.org).

Scripture quotations marked NLT are taken from the *Holy Bible, New Living Translation*, copyright © 1996, 2004. Used by permission of Tyndale House Publishers, Inc., Wheaton, Illinois 60189. All rights reserved.

Any Internet addresses (websites, blogs, etc.) and telephone numbers printed in this book are offered as a resource. They are not intended in any way to be or imply an endorsement by Zondervan, nor does Zondervan vouch for the content of these sites and numbers for the life of this book.

All rights reserved. No part of this publication may be reproduced, stored in a retrieval system, or transmitted in any form or by any means—electronic, mechanical, photocopy, recording, or any other—except for brief quotations in printed reviews, without the prior permission of the publisher.

Published in association with Kelley Norris and Melinda Doolittle Entertainment.

Packaged by Worthy Media. For subsidiary and foreign rights contact info@worthymedia.com.

Cover design: Chris Tobias, Tobias Design
Cover photography: Russ Harrington
Interior design: Inside Out Design & Typesetting

Printed in the United States of America

10 11 12 13 14 15 /DCI/ 23 22 21 20 19 18 17 16 15 14 13 12 11 10 9 8 7 6 5 4 3 2 1

This book is dedicated to
Marguerite Doolittle.

I truly believe that I have the best Mommy in the entire world and that I would not be the woman I am today without her guidance and example. I strive to be as selfless, giving, and inspiring as she has been to me. I grew up hearing these words every day: "Mommy loves her Baby." I just want to take this time to say, "Baby loves her Mommy!"

Contents

Foreword

I have received so much from being on *American Idol*, but one of the biggest blessings of that whole experience was getting to meet and become friends with Melinda Doolittle. We began as strangers, then were competitors, but quickly grew into friends. And now I don't know what I would do without her!

During the run of our season of *American Idol*, she was the oldest contestant and I was the youngest—and she soon became "Mama" to everyone! She was like a mother hen, helping, encouraging, and even scolding us when we needed it. And then I was lucky enough to have her a little more to myself when we became roommates at the Top 12 level of the show. I'll never forget those days. And I'm happy to report that three years later we still are constantly in touch (we're texting maniacs!)—and I get to spill my heart and hear her love back to me just like we did in the beginning. With this book, I've simply been inspired all over again!

Melinda has called her book *Beyond Me*, and I know that is where her amazing strength comes from. I loved reading about the adventures we shared on AI and seeing the same events from her unique perspective. But even more, I loved reading about the stories that were new to me—insights and memories from her childhood and growing-up years. It really made me see where she got all that wisdom!

I've read that happiness is elusive, but if you ever have the good fortune to meet Melinda, you'll know you've found it. I've never known anyone with so much joy in her life—and she's teaching me how to live that way too. I remember during the show—and even now when I need the reminder!—she would always say, "Don't worry about anyone else and what they're saying; just worry about you and be yourself." Now I know we've all heard that before, but for me, coming from Melinda—someone I so admire and respect—it had all the more power. These days, when I have young people come to me and ask for advice, I tell them the same thing. When you're yourself, people love you for you, and that is a great thing to know. As for Melinda, I know it's her faith and love of music and people that gives her that "joy of life." It's a remarkable quality that we all want. What an honor that Melinda is so willing to share her secrets to getting there—with me and everyone else on the journey.

You know, wherever either one of us goes, we get asked about everybody's favorite *Idol* judge, Simon Cowell. And we both answer the same thing (although it took me a lot longer than it took Melinda to get to this conclusion!): he's really just a supporter without a filter! We sometimes got angry at him for the way he said things, but as Melinda constantly reminded me, his ultimate goal was to help and bring out the very best in us.

Life can be tough as it tries to teach you things—think of it as Simon knocking you down so you can learn to get up again. As you take your place on whatever stage is before you, I know that Melinda's words will be as inspiring, encouraging, and helpful to you as they were to me. And we'll all make it through!

I love you, Melinda, and I'm so proud of you for putting all your best onto paper. Now the whole world can experience what I have—your fantastic sense of humor, your encouraging soul, your life wisdom, and your beautiful heart. Congratulations, my wonderful friend, on this amazing book.

And now, it is a great honor for me to introduce you to one of my favorite people in the world: Melinda Doolittle. I truly believe you will walk away from reading *Beyond Me* with a new and refreshed look at life, love, and your own pursuit of success and happiness!

Jordin Sparks

Acknowledgments

There are so many people who have contributed greatly to my life—too many to name—but I would like to give special thanks to:

- Steve Doolittle for being such a great Daddy and a wonderful example of a man.
- Kelley Norris for literally thinking for me and for being the best manager ever, as well as such an amazing friend.
- Ken Abraham for being patient with me and being such a joy to work with.

- Janet Kenyon, Chester and Roz Thompson, John Titta, Stacy Merida, Cedric and Victor Caldwell, Steve Crawford, Da'dra Greathouse, Michael W. Smith, Sheila E., CeCe Winans, University of Tulsa, and Belmont University for teaching me about the true heart of music.
- My family—the Dukes and the Doolittles—for showing me what unconditional love really is.
- Harriet, Pam, and Kalyn for the much needed girl talk.
- Doug Cordes for inviting me on the trip of a lifetime.
- Rob Birkhead and the entire team at Worthy Publishing for making this such a wonderful experience.
- Melinda's Backups™ for truly having my back no matter what.
- Malaria No More and The LEAGUE organization for showing me how easy it is to make a difference and for giving me the drive to never give up until a change is made.

1

Dream Big!

According to all the statistics, I am not supposed to succeed, and I am definitely not supposed to be happy. You see, I started my life as a shy, only child in a single-parent family; my mom and dad divorced when I was not quite one year old.

So how have I beaten the odds and defied the statistics? Why am I happy? Why do I feel like I have been blessed with success beyond my wildest dreams? To be truthful, it's beyond me.

I do know, however, that I haven't just sat back and let life throw at me whatever it will. Instead—and this has been key—I've always worked to find my way to life's next level. Hopefully, in the pages ahead, I'll be able to show you not only how to do the same but also why I believe success and happiness are more of a choice than merely a result of your circumstances.

Both my mom and dad are absolutely wonderful people. When I was growing up, I got to see my dad twice a year, and I spent the rest of the time with my mom. As she did for most things in my early life, Mom made me feel that having a single parent all to myself was the coolest thing ever!

Mom was my best friend. We had "girls' night" and slumber parties together, times when the two of us simply hung out and talked about life, big issues and small, and all that was going on in our world. One of our favorite activities was to put on our pajamas and have an *Anne of Green Gables* party, during which we watched the video for the umpteenth time and enjoyed it every bit as much as the first time. Mom also encouraged me to have my girlfriends over to our home, and she was quick to allow one or more of my friends to sleep over. She wanted to know my friends. Mom never allowed me to sleep over at the home of a friend unless she knew that the parents' lifestyle was consistent with her morals and values. Mom was always so innovative and creative when it came to our parties, too, coming up with all sorts of fun things to do. Although she never complained, I now realize that she had to be creative, since we lived on a very limited budget.

Nevertheless, not only did I get to have girls' nights with Mom and my friends on a regular basis at home, but I was also a jet-setter. Well, sort of. I got to fly—by myself—to visit my dad.

That was the way I was raised: *Figure out the best thing about a situation and run with it.* So, not surprisingly, that life principle has stuck with me—and come in very handy over the years.

I was also raised to believe I could be or do anything I put my mind to. And how do children figure out what they want to do or be? They try everything! Thankfully, my mom was up for the challenge, and she let me try almost any sport, instrument, or childhood activity at least once.

So What Were My Options?

As I considered those things that I enjoyed, I started with my closest role model.

Option 1: Be a Teacher

My mom has worked in schools all of my life. Mom has taught elementary, middle, and high school. She worked mainly in special education. She even worked in school administration for a while. School was Mom's life, so I figured it might be mine as well. I remember getting home from school before my mom, lining up my stuffed animals, and teaching them all the subjects. That's how I did my homework a lot of the time. I quickly realized, however, that I did not have the patience for teaching. Every time a stuffed animal got an answer wrong, I got so frustrated! Then I suspended the offending critter, and pretty soon, I would be down to one student. Teaching was out.

Option 2: Be an Ice-Skater

I loved watching ice-skating on television with my mom. I tried gliding and jumping around the room to show Mom my triple lutz, and she applauded and gave me my score. I probably should have figured out that ice-skating was not for me, considering the fact that she never gave me a perfect 10. But I asked to take skating lessons anyway. That dream faded as fast as it started. I quickly discovered that I had a fundamental problem with being an ice-skater: I can't stand to be cold. Ice-skating was out.

Option 3: Be a Dancer or a Gymnast

I should probably preface this with the fact that words really matter to my mom. She believes that words are powerful, that you receive what you say. Mom nicknamed me "Grace" in hopes that one day the name would stick and I would actually be graceful. Unfortunately, I was the kid who ran into everything, tripped over my own feet, and always found some new way to fall. Why I thought dancing or gymnastics would work is beyond me, but I tried. During the first dance class my mom observed, my fellow dancers and I were dancing around some kind of large column in the middle of the room. Of course, I was the only one to run into it—several times. Similarly, in my first gymnastics meet, I fell off the balance beam at least twice; my highest score was a 6.3 out of a possible 10. Dancing and gymnastics were out.

Option 4: Be a Singer

After I had stumbled through bunches of activities, the one thing I absolutely could not get enough of at the end of the day was music. First, I tried playing instruments. The only time Mom ever flinched about me taking lessons was when I wanted to play the saxophone: "You know, Melinda, the flute is a little more delicate. The saxophone is really loud."

I tried the saxophone, and not only was it really loud, but I was really bad.

I later switched to the flute and did fairly well, landing a first-chair position in our school band. I finally found something I was good at, but it wasn't enough. It wasn't my passion.

Now, my mom and dad had very different views about the kind of music I should listen to. My mom played only Christian music in our home. My dad, on the other hand, wanted me to hear the reason he had started playing drums so many years ago—when Motown was in its prime. I immediately fell in love with Gladys Knight, Stevie Wonder, Michael Jackson, and so many more. A new dream blossomed within me. I wanted to be a *singer!*

There was only one problem with that. I was tone-deaf. As much as I loved music, it did not love me. It wasn't that I didn't try; I tried my best. I remember how excited I was when I finally got into a choir. Come to find out, they loved my charisma, so they put me in the middle of the group, but they specifically requested that I not sing, that I simply lip sync. "Just move your lips, Melinda," the director would say. "Stand there in the middle of the group and mouth the words, but please don't let any sound come out."

I was happy to do it, though, because I was still considered a member of the choir, and I loved every second! However, as far as my choir directors were concerned, for me, singing was out.

I did not see it that way. As any tone-deaf person knows, *I* was not the problem. When I sang alone and a cappella, I thought I was pretty good. The problems started when people and music were added. For some reason, their voices and instruments did not want to adapt to my pitch. So I quickly learned that if I were going to be part of a choir, I would have to sacrifice singing out loud. That was okay with me. I was the best at the "hand-ography," and my huge smile contributed to performances that were loved by our parents and friends in the audience. I was content . . . for a while.

I remember the day everything changed for me. It was the summer before seventh grade, and I was shopping for shoes with my mom. Neither of us really liked to shop, so it wasn't fun at all, and I was looking for any distraction. Just then, a Whitney Houston song came on over the store's speaker system, and not only did we stop shopping, but everyone in the store stopped to listen. Whitney's voice was so commanding and beautiful. The moment lasted only a few seconds, but it seemed like forever.

As everyone went back to shopping, I started imagining and dreaming. I don't even recall the rest of the shopping trip. All I remember is getting home and telling my mom that I wanted to sing for real! I wanted a voice to come out of me that made people stop and listen.

My mom searched to find words that would not discourage me from my dream, but still be honest. I believe her exact reply was "Baby, you're going to have to pray—*HARD!*"

So I did. I prayed harder than I had ever prayed. I promised God that when He did this for me, if people stopped and listened, I would represent Him well. Then I set a goal. I decided I wanted to be able to sing with music at the Fusion talent show. Fusion was the name of my youth group at Rhema Bible Church in Tulsa, Oklahoma. I learned so much at church about having strong faith and dreaming big, so what better place to debut my new voice?

I had the dream, I had the faith, I had the venue. Now, I needed the song. My mom and I have always loved the song "Oh, the Blood of Jesus." So we went to the store to find the soundtrack for my favorite version, one I had heard on *Gospel Bill*, a television show I loved as a child. Once the song was picked, the only thing left to do was practice, practice, practice! I practiced for a full month to get ready. I was living and breathing that song.

Then the day came. My youth pastor, Kent Booth, and the staff were kind enough to let me be a part of the show even though they had heard me sing in the past and knew the potential for disaster. It was so great to have them believe me when I said, "I can do it this time."

All I remember about that event is stepping onto the stage and hearing the music start. I closed my eyes, took a deep breath, and began to sing. I don't recall anything about the actual performance, but when it was over, I opened my eyes and saw all of Fusion on their feet, clapping and cheering. My mom was in the back of the room, crying tears of joy.

When I got home later that evening, my mom told me that some of the youth leaders had gone to Kent and expressed their concern that I had been allowed to lip sync in the talent show. He had just laughed and explained to them that the quiet girl with the big smile had been singing for real! I haven't stopped smiling or singing since.

Because I have had some dreams come true, I love encouraging other people to dream, to open their hearts and minds and see what they can do and what God can do in and through them. Nowadays I like to tell people that I meet after my concerts, "Dream big!" That's how I sign my photos and my albums, usually adding a reference to my favorite Bible verse, Ephesians 3:20. I quote it to anyone who will listen:

> Now to Him Who, by . . . [the action of His] power that is at work within us, is able to . . . do superabundantly, far over and above all that we [dare] ask or think [infinitely beyond our highest prayers, desires, thoughts, hopes, or dreams]. (AMP)

Let me tell you why I know this verse is absolutely true. After that talent show, not only could I sing with other people and musicians, but I could hear harmonies, I could make them up on my own, and the sound of my voice was more powerful than I could have ever imagined.

Years later, I walked into a recording session in Nashville, Tennessee, to sing background vocals for a project Israel Houghton was producing. The songs were for a church in Texas that had just hired a new worship leader. My mouth dropped open when he came into the studio.

It was Kent Booth. We hugged, and Kent said, "Melinda, what in the world are you doing here?"

"I'm singing background on your album." Kent wasn't aware of it, but by that time in my career, I had already sung on dozens of albums.

"Wow! Did you ever dream in a million years that you'd be doing this for a living?"

Of course I did! I'd dreamed it over and over again.

2

Say Three Nice Things

Sometimes we say words—good, bad, uplifting, or nasty—and think they will simply disappear into thin air. But I was raised to believe that our words matter, that the words we say have the power to build someone up or tear that person down. Mom held to the principle: *Say three nice things.* "Baby, if you're going to say something bad about someone, you need to say three good things about that person first."

Sometimes it was hard to come up with three nice things—especially if I had had a bad day at school and my teacher had treated me unfairly. Mom would say, "Well, tell me three good things about your teacher first." Consequently,

I never got to say a lot of the bad things I may have thought! Of course, her advice was irritating to me at the time, but I have discovered a lot of wisdom in my mother's bits of simple, commonsense truth. In fact, a lot of Mom's sayings have helped me develop an optimistic outlook on life and contributed greatly to my success.

Even today, interviewers will sometimes get frustrated with me because I choose to say three nice things first rather than begin with the negatives. It's not my fault that most interviews are so short that I only have time to get to the nice stuff! The question I am asked most often is "What is Simon Cowell really like?" Knowing Simon as the sometimes painfully honest, difficult-to-please judge on *American Idol*, interviewers expect that they will finally get me to say something negative. Instead, they are shocked to find out that Simon is my teddy bear. Simon's underlying purpose is to jolt you into doing your best. He simply doesn't have a filter, and he never learned to start with three nice things.

The Gift Everyone Needs

When I started eighth grade, my church hired a new youth pastor. His name was Jimmie Pierce, and he was wonderful! Soon after he arrived, he came up with the idea of giving out engraved trophies to members of the youth group he felt had positively impacted the lives of others. Since I was not at all athletic, I had never before received a trophy, so I thought this was amazing. However, I couldn't think of anything I had done to warrant an award. So imagine my surprise when my name was called to receive the Barnabas Award.

I thought, *What? Who is Barnabas, why am I like him, and why couldn't I get an award with a pretty name?* As I walked up to receive my trophy, Jimmie explained that the name *Barnabas* means "the son of encouragement." Then I understood.

One of my favorite things is seeing the look on someone's face when he or she realizes that he is unique, that she is needed, or that they are completely capable of doing whatever they set their mind on. So I spent a lot of time telling people just that. I didn't realize, until that moment, how important that encouragement can be to someone else.

My goal is to encourage everyone I can, because we all need it. From the person who is marvelously successful, to the person who has suffered some setbacks, to the individual who is down-and-out and struggling to get back on his or her feet, encouragement is the gift we all can use.

Ironically, it takes very little effort or talent to encourage someone. All you need is a willing heart. Sometimes just a smile, a friendly hello, or a kind compliment will impart such meaning and value to another person's life. But you have to be willing to offer that encouragement with love and a genuine desire to help.

During the *American Idol* competition, I did my best to say positive things to my fellow contestants. They called me "Mama" since, at twenty-nine, I was the oldest person in the competition. I tended to regard the younger contestants as my "babies," so although I was in the competition to win, I wanted to help them as much as possible.

Just being a performer on that show is stressful and tiring, so for a vocalist, the very real possibility of your voice betraying you looms large during every performance. To help me avoid that, one of my friends had given me a *Pro Vox* DVD and CD series. I took this tremendous vocal training tool to the competition with me, and naturally I shared the warm-up exercises with my fellow singers. Each night, right before *American Idol* went on the air "live," some of us gathered in a room to do warm-ups together before going on stage.

We were really a close-knit group during *American Idol, Season Six*. In fact, the producers said we were more like a family than any group they'd had so far. We helped one another with song selection and performance feedback, and we often provided a friendly shoulder to cry on.

On *Idol*, success is not always about performing songs you like; it is more important to do songs that you perform well. Sometimes a contestant would ask my opinion about a song he or she planned to sing on the show. I always kept Mom's advice in mind: *Say three nice things.* I answered kindly but honestly even if I knew my answer wasn't what the person wanted to hear: "That's a cool song, but can you make it your own?" Of course, we second-guessed every decision we made about our song choices: "Is this the best song for me? Will the judges like it? Will America like it?" You don't always get your first choice of songs, so we tried to find several potential numbers for each of us to sing. For a variety of reasons—mostly copyright issues but maybe another competitor had already selected the same song—we sometimes ended up singing a second or third choice. That's why it was wise to prepare several songs just in case. It's great to remember how supportive we were of one another even though we were competing. We became like a large, diverse family.

Speak the Truth in Love

Understand, speaking positively does not mean that you avoid necessary confrontations or that you are afraid to speak the truth. I saw such truth speaking when I watched *This Is It,* the Michael Jackson documentary. My favorite part of the movie was when Michael was rehearsing with his band and they weren't getting it right. He brought them together to explain what he needed changed and what he expected of them. But when correcting the band members, Michael emphasized that he was saying it in love—"L-O-V-E."

One of my pet peeves is when people intentionally hurt others with their words.

During *Idol*, one of the contestants would say things that he knew would upset his fellow contestants. Right before his competitor went on stage, he'd say something like "I was just reading in one of the blogs that you don't look your best in a form-fitting dress." Of course the contestant was about to step onstage in a form-fitting dress.

That's just mean. And totally unnecessary. I witnessed him doing something similar on several occasions, always right before a contestant was about to step on stage, and I quickly realized that the perpetrator was using his negative words as a strategy to sabotage another singer's performance. Since I regarded the young singers on the show as "my babies," the next time I heard him make a negative comment to a fellow contestant, I confronted him about it. As we were about to step on stage, I positioned myself right in front of him. With the *American Idol* theme music playing in the background, I didn't have time to come up with three nice things. Instead,

I looked him right in the eyes and said, "You do this one more time, and I'm coming after you. I love you because Jesus said I have to, but I don't like you."

The lights came up, and we heard announcer Ryan Seacrest saying, "Ladies and gentlemen, our American idols!"

Although I may have been justified in my action, there was probably a better way to handle the situation. Maybe I should have taken Michael Jackson's lead and ended the encounter with more "L-O-V-E." The stresses and strains of life sometimes make it difficult to look at the positive, but attempting to say three nice things can at least steer you in the right direction.

Why do some people feel it necessary to point out the mistakes, sins, or failures of others, often ridiculing or gossiping about them, rather than trying to say positive things? Maybe the most caustic critics were raised that way themselves, so now they feel compelled to cut other people down to size so they can feel better about their own shortcomings. Regardless of the reason, it is wrong.

Our society today seems obsessed with building someone up only to see how quickly we can tear that person down. But it's really not hard to be kind and encouraging. Once you get into the habit of attempting to say three nice things, you find your mind taking you there rather than toward negative, destructive comments.

So make it a practice to stop and think before speaking. I am always better off if I pause and take a deep breath before saying something negative: I give my brain a moment to catch up with my mouth. I recently saw a simple acronym to apply to my speaking: remember to THINK.

T—Is what you are about to say True?

H—Is it Helpful?

I—Is it Inspiring?

N—Is it Necessary?

K—Is it Kind?[1]

Perhaps, as the old adage advises, if you can't say anything nice, you'd be better off saying nothing at all. Better still, attempt to be positive in all your conversations. Seek to say three nice things. Other people will be encouraged, you'll feel better about yourself, and your heavenly Father will be pleased.

1 David Jeremiah, "Think," *Turning Point Magazine & Devotional*, October 2009, 36.

3

Be Prepared

Part of being prepared for life is to always do your best. I learned this lesson from Coach Blankenship, the football coach at Union High School in Tulsa, Oklahoma, who also happened to be my biology teacher.

On one of my test papers, he wrote, "See me"—which is definitely not something a student ever wants to read. When I went to see Coach Blankenship after class, he asked me, "Why aren't you applying yourself to your studies?"

"Well, I don't really care about biology. I'm applying myself to my music. I don't need math or science to sing."

Coach Blankenship did something you will rarely see in

a public school. He pulled out a Bible from his desk drawer and read aloud the passage in Colossians 3:23 that calls us to do all of our work as unto the Lord.

I had never thought about my schoolwork in that way before.

"Plus," he said, "you'll need more than just good grades in your music classes. You'll need a high overall GPA to get a scholarship and study music in college. If you apply yourself here and do your best, you will be able to go to any college you want."

I took my teacher's words to heart. Thanks to Coach Blankenship's encouragement, I worked hard for the remainder of my high-school years. I poured myself into my studies, and I joined any choir that would have me. I loved choral arrangements and music theory, and I even auditioned for Oklahoma's All-State Choir. In addition to being in the All-State Choir each of the three years I was eligible, I received a full-ride music and academic scholarship to the University of Tulsa, where I majored in classical music.

I attended the University of Tulsa for two years and learned so much, but as my sophomore year came to a close, I sensed that I was ready for something else. Classical music was beautiful, but I wanted to study other styles also.

I began looking at various schools that might have a strong

music program. I was leaning toward the University of Miami, but then a friend told me about the Music Business program at Belmont University in Nashville. Mom visited Belmont with me, and we both instantly fell in love with it. The campus was much smaller than Tulsa, and everyone was so friendly; it seemed as though the students and faculty knew one another by name. Classes were smaller, and the school boasted state-of-the-art recording studios as well. Mom was impressed, and I was too. Although I'm sure Mom was somewhat sad that I'd be moving so far away if I were to attend Belmont, she also understood that my time at Tulsa had come to a close.

My transition could not have been more perfect. Even though I didn't know anyone at Belmont before arriving on campus, once there, I met a woman who would become one of my best friends, Janet Kenyon. Janet was a young music professor at Belmont, and she was an amazing instructor. Everyone wanted to take classes from her. One class she taught, Pop-Rock Styles, proved tremendously helpful to me, because it taught me how to sing various styles of music without blowing out my vocal cords. Janet's class was invaluable to me, teaching me about breath control, blend, and consistency so I could replicate what I sang when it came time to "stack" vocals, to record one layer of background vocals on top of another. She also taught about artistry and how to choose material that best fits my voice. It's easy now to see how God was leading me even then, how He was preparing me for what I would experience on *American Idol*, where I would be challenged to sing a wide variety of styles and find songs that really worked for my voice.

At Belmont, I also studied with Sandra Dudley, a private voice instructor. Sandra is an excellent jazz singer, and she taught me all sorts of secrets to hearing and forming parts. She directed a Belmont vocal ensemble known as Jazzmin. When I auditioned for the group, she invited me to join them. Simply learning the unusual parts we were to sing expanded my vocal limits and "stretched my ear," helping me to hear potential parts in a fresh way. Sandra was also the first person to tell me, "Melinda, your vibrato needs to calm down."

My classical training greatly influenced the amount of vibrato I had allowed in my voice. While Sandra appreciated that quality, she knew it wouldn't work for most contemporary styles of music. But before I bumped into Sandra's rather blunt analysis, no one had ever mentioned the problems with my vibrato, so I thought I was doing just fine. Sandra's realistic appraisal poked a huge hole in my idealistic balloon.

"I really like your tone," Sandra encouraged, "but we need to get your vibrato under control. Start listening to some artists who have a faster vibrato and study how they use their breathing to enhance their singing while they limit the vibrato."

At first, Sandra's frank suggestions upset and offended me. After all, I had received a full scholarship to Tulsa and a partial scholarship even as a transfer student to Belmont, so I felt confident that my singing ability had attracted some attention. But after I listened to some recordings of my singing voice, I knew she was right. I decided then and there, "I'm going to work on fixing my vibrato." I also realized that I had a ton to learn about music and singing.

I completed a commercial music program with an emphasis on music business. After graduating from Belmont, I wanted to continue my vocal lessons. By then Janet had opened her own studio, Kenyon Artist Development, so I started studying there, and she continued to expand my musical horizons. Janet is an amazing vocalist herself who still works on the road and in the studio, so she knows what it takes to perform under pressure on stage and to sing all day in a recording studio without tiring your voice. Major recording companies send their artists to her so she can help them perform better and communicate with their audiences more effectively.

One of the best things Janet taught me was how to sing when I am not feeling one hundred percent. No singer is able to perform at the top of his or her vocal ability on *every* occasion, especially when on tour for several months from one city to the next (or one country to the next), night after night. So Janet emphasizes warming up vocally before every performance. I learned that failing to properly warm up with vocal exercises can damage an artist's voice, resulting in vocal cord nodules or other debilitating throat problems that can prematurely end a career.

Janet has developed a CD and DVD program known as *A Pro Vox Workout* that teaches singers how to control their voice—everything from projection of the sound to flexibility and power in your singing. Janet's DVD has definitely become a lifesaver for me. As I mentioned, I even took my *Pro Vox* CDs with me when I went to Los Angeles to appear on *American Idol*, and I shared them with anyone who wanted to use them. Before long, everyone in Season Six knew about *Pro Vox*, and some even used Janet's program to warm up before going on air.

Looking back, I now see that each step of the way—each step at the University of Tulsa, at Belmont, and at Kenyon Artist Development—was important to my preparation. I wasn't simply attending college or studying voice; I was forging a career, a career I wasn't aware of, but one God had been planning for me even before I was born!

One prime example of how being prepared helped take

me to the next level in my music was my first big break as a background singer. Cyndy Pasley, a friend and fellow background singer, worked frequently with renowned record producers Cedric and Victor Caldwell. One day Cyndy said to me, "I want to take you with me to the Caldwells' studio. I think they really need to meet you, so come and hang out with me while I work. Just know that before we leave, I am going to make you sing."

Even though I was completely nervous, I went along with Cyndy and observed her amazing work. Listening to Cyndy record with the Caldwells, I began to second-guess myself, because I had never done anything like what I saw Cyndy doing. But when they were done recording, Cyndy—as promised—had me sing "Amazing Grace" for Cedric and Victor. I guess they liked what they heard, because when I left that night, Cedric handed me a CD of the song "Jesus, You're Beautiful," a cut he was producing for one of my favorite artists, CeCe Winans. He also gave me a CD by the Irish vocalist Enya. "Go home and listen to these," Cedric said, "and see if you can figure out some Enya-style background vocals for 'Jesus, You're Beautiful.' Then, come back tomorrow and let me hear what you've come up with."

I went home, listened to the CDs, and worked on putting together the background parts. The following day, I went back to Cedric and let him hear what I had dreamed up.

Cedric listened as I sang, and when I finished, he asked, "How much time do you have today?"

"Well, actually, my schedule happens to be open."

"Okay, good. Jump in the booth and let's record."

I didn't have time to freak out about the fact that I was getting ready to sing on CeCe Winans' project and working with one of the most respected producers in the business. We went to work immediately and "stacked" the parts, recording eight separate tracks for first the alto, then the tenor, and then the soprano parts. When we were done, Cedric handed me a CD of another song and said, "Next week, same time."

I ended up recording most of the background vocals on eight songs for CeCe's award-winning *Throne Room* album. The album's success confirmed my entrance into the exclusive club of Nashville studio musicians. Had I not worked hard studying different styles of music, matching tone and timbre, and learning to hear harmonies, I would not have been ready to walk through the door that God opened for me that day.

More and more opportunities to sing background came along, and I was determined to be as prepared as possible. Granted, sometimes there's no way to know what to expect in a certain situation, so you feel like you cannot really prepare, but there are little things you can do that make a difference. I remember, for instance, getting called to do a studio session one day, and they said we were to start at 10:00 a.m. I didn't know what kind of song we were doing, what the producer was like, or who the project was for. The *only* thing I knew was the time and place, so I was determined to show up on time. I had no idea that something that small would make such an impact. When I walked in the door of the studio, the producer looked shocked.

"It's only 9:45," he said. "I wasn't expecting anyone here until at least 10:15." I started to apologize for arriving so early, and he stopped me. "Your being on time not only shows me you are reliable, but it also saves me money." From that day forward, the producer used me for almost all of his sessions. While I would love to say he kept hiring me for my voice, I really think it was more because he knew he could depend on me to be there on time and ready to work.

Even now, I still like to walk into a place on time and be prepared for whatever the particular event requires. It means less stress for me and for everyone else involved. An important part of being prepared is punctuality: show up on time and be ready to work.

Life Lessons on the Road

Looking back, I now realize that another key part of my musical preparation took place outside both the classroom and the recording studio. Prior to moving to Nashville, I didn't realize that it was possible to make a living as a background singer for other artists. "Do you mean they actually pay you to sing with them?" I naively asked my friends.

They rolled their eyes as if to say, "Oh, Melinda, you have so much to learn!" And, of course, I did.

One of the places where I found a home away from home was my local church. Like many churches in Nashville, the congregation with whom I worshipped was the home church for several nationally known music artists. One day, I noticed in the church bulletin that the group Anointed was holding auditions for a singer. One of their singers, Ne'Cee, had decided to take some time off as she anticipated having a baby, so Anointed was searching for Ne'Cee's replacement.

At first I thought, *No way would I want to audition for Anointed!* I really do not enjoy auditions—I literally shake while I sing at auditions—but the more I thought about it, the more something inside me said, "Do it!" So I became determined to try. I knew the only way I would go through with the audition was for me to tell a friend who would hold me accountable. So, I told my roommate, Rebecca, and she definitely held me to it.

I had grown up listening to Anointed's music, so I knew their material. On top of that, Ne'Cee had been the alto of the group, and that was my favorite part to sing. Plus Steve and Da'dra Crawford, the brother/sister backbone of Anointed, attended the same church as I did, so I should have been more comfortable at the audition. But I was horribly nervous. I went to Soundcheck, a rehearsal hall in Nashville, and I was so rattled that my hand kept shaking as I held the microphone and tried to sing into it. Steve and Da'dra were kind and encouraging, but the audition was not a pleasant experience. I sang the solo, and then Steve and Da'dra asked me to sing a piece with them. At the close of the audition, Steve said, "You will hear from us even if it is a no." But a few weeks went by, and I heard nothing.

I must have been so bad, they didn't even want to call me back, I thought.

Little did I know that the group had decided that rather than replace Ne'Cee, they'd simply bring on a new background singer—me. When I was leaving church one Sunday, Da'dra noticed me and said, "You shook all the way through, yet there was something special about that audition, so we will be calling you. I understand getting nervous, but we want to take you on the road with us."

I was ecstatic. I started meeting with the group in Steve's basement and working on harmonies with them. They were so good to work with, and they treated me so well. I sang alto and tenor, and my friend Jovaun, another vocalist, sang soprano. Later, when Jovaun started her family, another friend of mine, Missi, joined us.

The first time I ever got on a tour bus was with Anointed. I crawled up into my bunk on the bus, and I was home. I slept so well that night as the hum of the bus tires rolling down the highway lulled me to sleep.

To me, everything about being on tour was exciting, from the daily sound check . . . to the concerts at night . . . to meeting people after the shows as I worked at our merchandise tables. I loved it all! I had sung in studios, but doing a "live" concert every night was much different. After all, there were people out there in those auditoriums! I was excited to see them, but at first I was so shy that I attempted to hide behind Da'dra on stage. I'd strategically position myself so most of the audience couldn't see me in the shadows. Slowly, I became more comfortable performing in front of a crowd, and I eventually came out of hiding. I sang with Anointed for five years, and I learned much about performing as well as about the business aspects of music. Steve and Da'dra were the consummate teachers, too, constantly instructing simply by their examples.

"If you ever want to do this as a career," Steve or Da'dra would tell me, "know what you are getting into and know what is important to you." I had attended Belmont University to learn the business of music, and I will always be grateful for that opportunity, but working with Anointed taught me the practical side of the music business.

Of all the lessons that Anointed taught me, my favorite was the importance of being the same offstage as we were onstage. They didn't change their personae to go on stage; they were simply and always real people. Nor did they treat people differently away from the concert venues. They treated everyone—concert promoters, stagehands, waitresses in the restaurants, everyone—with respect and kindness. Even within our group, nobody expected or received superstar treatment, but we were all treated very well.

By the same token, Steve and Da'dra expected us to treat other people well. They recognized that everything we said or did represented Anointed and, ultimately, represented our Lord God about whom we sang. If one of us spoke to anyone harshly or inappropriately, Steve or Da'dra was quick to gently remind us, "That's not how we talk to people here." They never yelled or made a scene; they simply encouraged us: "We don't put other people down. We need to keep our tone positive, friendly, and upbeat."

I also learned from Anointed that the better we treated the people who brought us in to sing, the more likely we were to be invited back for another performance. That might seem like a given to you, but unfortunately treating one's host well is not as common as you might think. Although I suppose it's easy as an artist to become arrogant, pushy, and demanding, Anointed was just the opposite. They were always kind and gracious. Consequently, concert promoters, pastors, and civic leaders wanted to work with them to inspire their audiences. It was a win-win situation.

Although I didn't realize it at the time, Anointed was teaching me what sort of an artist I wanted to become. As I watched how they handled all sorts of situations, I observed in everyday life what it means to be a performing artist who is a Christian, not simply a Christian performing artist. Anointed kept their faith an integral part of their lives. They understood the importance of maintaining an active, growing relationship with Christ. Steve led us in Bible studies on the bus, and I loved watching videos of great church services in my bunk. Anointed became my family. We had so much fun together. We laughed, cried, and prayed together. Steve and Da'dra were my brother and sister as well as my mentors.

Although Anointed was my priority, I branched out and worked with other artists as our concert schedule allowed. In the music business, it's always important to have multiple streams of income flowing, so when I wasn't working with Anointed, I also sang for both Martha Munizzi and a group called RiZen. I kept singing background in the studio as well. I rarely took a day off.

Often aspiring artists approach me and ask, "How can I get started in the music business?" or "How can I do what you are doing?" I tell them three things: Dream big, pray hard, and be prepared.

Dreaming big is important, because if you don't see yourself doing what you want to do, you can be fairly sure that nobody else will imagine you doing it either. So set your sights high and post your goals right in front of you on your "faith wall."

Praying is important too. And by praying hard, I don't mean yelling at God. On the other hand, I also don't mean mumbling vague, ambiguous prayers, simply hinting to God that you would like to do something great. I believe in specific, consistent, and intense prayer. When you pray and follow God's directions, He can open the right doors for you at the right time.

But you must be prepared. Know your craft, practice it, study it, and hone your skills to the best of your ability; then let God take care of the rest. When I first began singing background, I took lessons all the time, and I listened constantly to all sorts of background vocals. I was determined to take my career to the next level. For that to happen, I had to quickly learn the styles of a wide variety of singers. In the middle of a session, a producer sometimes said something like "Give me a little India.Arie vibe on this and mix it with a bit of how Macy Gray does her background vocals." The producer wasn't going to wait for me to go home and learn the part. I had to know the craft.

From the time I was old enough to notice, I watched my daddy demonstrate how preparedness can help you in your career. His example taught me about the importance of honing your craft, setting goals, visualizing the outcome, and identifying any roadblocks that might occur. He also taught me that, regardless of the career you pursue, it is vital that you work hard to excel.

If all you do is dream big and pray hard, but you never study, practice, and prepare, it's presumptuous to ask God to do the rest. He expects us to work at what we do, to be ready, so when the opportunity comes, we can step right into it and enjoy the benefits of our preparation, coupled with His grace.

4

Pay It Forward

The movie *Pay It Forward* is one of my favorites. If you haven't seen it, I definitely recommend taking the time to experience the film. I promise I won't give away the plot, but the premise involves a young boy's social studies project. He decides that if each person "paid it forward," or helped someone with something he or she could not achieve alone, we could change the world. He suggested it could start by one person paying it forward to three people. Then, each of those three would choose three others to help, and the impact would increase exponentially. Before you knew it, your simple acts of kindness would not only affect your city, but they could change your state, your country, and possibly even our world.

One of the people who best models the "pay it forward" concept for me is Roz Thompson, my music mom. I went to college with her son Akil. He was one of the best musicians in the school, so I should have known that he had good music genes! The day I met Miss Roz, I was in rehearsals to sing background for Belmont University's Commercial Music Showcase. However, when Roz came into the rehearsal room, we weren't singing; we were learning choreography. Knowing I wasn't the most graceful person, I was quite embarrassed to see an observer in the audience. And I was completely caught off guard when she approached me after rehearsal and offered me a job!

And this wasn't just any job. Without even knowing whether or not I sang professionally, Roz Thompson invited me to be part of a recording session. I mentioned not having experience and not having a car. She said that was no problem, that she would send her husband to pick me up, so I timidly accepted my first professional session. Miss Roz would later tell me that, as she sat in her seat watching us rehearse the showcase choreography, something told her to ask me to join the session. I'm so glad she did.

The day of the recording session, I rode to the studio

in complete silence with Mr. Chester, Roz's husband. A few weeks later, I realized that I had been given a ride by *the* Chester Thompson, drummer for Genesis, Phil Collins, Frank Zappa, and many other highly acclaimed music artists.

I arrived before most of the other singers on the project did, and Roz was waiting for me. I could tell she was excited about the day as she introduced me to each arriving vocalist and provided me with some tidbits of information about each one. I soon discovered that not only was my first session for an award-winning song, "My Deliverer," but it was being produced by Rick Elias as a tribute to the recently deceased Rich Mullins. I was enormously honored to be a part of the ensemble. My honor turned to awe when I walked into the studio and saw that in addition to Miss Roz, I would be singing with Nicole C. Mullen, George Pendergrass of the group Acappella, Sarah and Billy Gaines, and Ken "Scat" Springs. They welcomed me as though I were a studio regular.

Together our group created an amazingly rich, powerful sound. We worked together for about three hours, and I had the time of my life!

When we finished the song, we all filed into Rick's office. Rick handed each of us a check for singing on the project.

I looked at the amount on the check, and my eyes opened wide in surprise. *There must be some mistake*, I thought. I took the check back to the producer and said, "Mr. Elias, I only sang on one song, so I think my check might be wrong."

He chuckled and answered, "No ma'am. It's exactly right!" That was the first time I realized that not only do people in Nashville get paid to sing, but that this was what I wanted to do for a living. I'll always be grateful to Miss Roz for taking a chance on an unknown singer. What faith she must have had! Her example has inspired me to keep my heart open, as well as my eyes and ears, as I look for opportunities to help someone else realize his or her dreams.

After that first session, Miss Roz continued to hire me to sing background vocals for various artists, and she and Mr. Chester became like surrogate parents to me. To this day, I go to them for advice on all sorts of matters, but especially advice about music.

Eating It Forward!

Some of my favorite memories are of hosting student dinners at my house after graduating from college. I invited college students from Belmont, Middle Tennessee State University, Tennessee State University, and my church for an annual holiday dinner between Thanksgiving and Christmas. Most of my close friends know that I don't cook very often, so suffice it to say, these students were brave. Even when I did venture into the kitchen, I cooked only the entrees I was comfortable preparing, which means we had the exact same dinner every year. When I wanted to change the menu, I called on Steve Crawford (yes, the singer from Anointed) to cook. If you know Steve or ever have the pleasure of meeting him in the future, please ask him for food. I know it sounds weird, but it will be the most wonderful meal *ever!*

I obviously love food, but the meal was not my favorite part of these gatherings. I loved the conversation. We felt comfortable talking about anything. The students could ask me whatever they wanted about issues that came up in life, school, or work. Sometimes I knew the answer, sometimes I didn't, but hopefully the fact that they had a place to freely express themselves, someplace where they could be honest about what they were dealing with, helped them know they weren't alone.

The students especially enjoyed hearing me tell about my "faith walls." On my walls at college, I used to have posters of artists for whom I wanted to sing background. Every morning, I'd wake up, look at the images on my faith walls, and say, "Someday I'm going to sing for you."

Over time, I eventually sang with or for each of those

artists whose picture I once had hanging on my wall. I kept my goals in front of me, so I could remind myself every day, "This is where I am going." I admonished the students to do the same. To this day, a lot of my "babies" have their own faith walls, and they have inspired others to do something similar. They are paying it forward.

Giving Back

The first Christmas that I can remember vividly, I was living in St. Louis. I was with my mom, and she decided we were going to share the spirit of giving. Now mind you, I was only about six years old, so I was very much into *getting* instead of *giving*. I was not happy with my mom for dragging me out of the house, into the cold, to go serve food to people who lived outside and might have germs, but I didn't have a choice. Mom had already volunteered us to work with Larry Rice Ministries, the organization that was sponsoring the outreach. I went reluctantly, but my mood changed quickly when I saw little girls like me and mommies just like mine. These weren't people with germs; these were families excited about having a warm place to rest, food to eat, and gifts for their children. I had no idea how their gratefulness would affect me, but I never complained about participating any year after that. Instead, I was so excited about meeting all of the families, watching them get their food and gifts, and being a part of their Christmas each year. My mom and I continued to participate in the annual Christmas outreach until we moved from St. Louis when I was ten.

Learning the truth that giving affects the giver as well as the recipient made a profound impression in my life. Now I actually look for opportunities to pay it forward, especially when children are involved.

The LEAGUE

I love children! I love to see them smile, hear them laugh, and listen to their views on life. So when I got a call asking me to help launch The LEAGUE, I was very excited. This program—started by former Secretary of Education Margaret Spellings—goes into schools, mainly in the New York area, and teaches children about good character traits and community service. It is amazing to hear the children's ideas about which character traits they feel are most important—truthfulness and encouragement. Thanks to The LEAGUE, the elementary-aged children are learning how to put these traits into action in their homes and communities. I was honored to have been part of the launch of the program, and I am so happy that The LEAGUE is still going strong and that children are continuing to make a huge difference in their schools and neighborhoods.

Everyone Can Do Something

As a result of participating on *American Idol*, I now have a more visible platform to talk with people about making a difference in our world. I've discovered that most people really want to make a difference; they just haven't found a good way to do it. The problems seem too big, so overwhelming. What can one person do?

Actually, one person can do a lot. I was privileged to be a part of the first-ever "Idol Gives Back" television show. The idea was to use two episodes of *American Idol* as a telethon to raise money for underprivileged children in Africa and the U.S., particularly those affected by Hurricane Katrina. For the first fifty million people who voted during the program, News Corp pledged ten cents each, up to $5 million. More than $30 million was raised when the show and the results show aired "live" on April 24-25, 2007. Corporate sponsors such as Coca-Cola, Ford, MySpace, and others also contributed, boosting the total to more than $70 million as of May 1, 2007.

Because of that show, I became involved with the organization Malaria No More. Prior to the "Idol Gives Back" program, the executive producers of the show called us artists into an office where we watched some videos that were going to run on *Idol* that week. These videos gave us a better understanding of the devastating effects of malaria on so many African children. The producers wanted us to know what we were singing about and why we were trying to raise money for people we had never met. I was shocked. I had no idea that malaria was such a huge problem or that it affected a million children every year, many of whom would die simply because they didn't have a mosquito net to hang over their beds to prevent infection. Once I saw those kids' faces, I said, "I'm in! How can I help?"

Almost immediately following the conclusion of the sixth season of *American Idol*, we began rehearsals for the follow-up tour in which the top ten finalists would perform at fifty-nine concerts in various cities around the United States. One day, I received a phone call from Simon Fuller, the program's chief executive. "I'd like to invite you to go to Africa with Laura Bush," he offered. "The trip is during your tour rehearsals, but I can arrange for you to be excused for the five days. If you're up for working really hard on your rehearsals, I'd like for you to go."

I nearly screamed, "Yes!" I had always dreamed of going to Africa someday, but to go along as part of then-First Lady Laura Bush's entourage was more exciting than I could have imagined. I met with Martin Edlund from Malaria No More, and he briefed me about the organization's work in Zambia. He also informed me that I had to get all the usual vaccinations and anti-malaria medications before the whirlwind trip. I'm pretty scared of needles, but we would be traveling right into mosquito-infested areas, and we dared not go in unprotected.

Martin described the bed nets treated with insecticide that they provided to the Zambian people and explained that it was important to teach the people how to use the simple protective devices. Sadly, in previous efforts, many people received the nets but left them unopened right near their beds as mosquitoes carrying malaria bit them while they slept. In Zambia, another child dies from malaria every thirty seconds.

I embarked from Los Angeles along with Sophia, a representative of 19 Management, an artist management company that represents *American Idol* contestants. Landing in Washington, D.C., I received my first post-*Idol* taste of being recognized. Right there in the airport, people called out my name, and I waved in response. It wasn't until Sophia and I boarded our flight for Johannesburg, South Africa, that I was able to relax. Eighteen hours later we landed, and as we were going up the crowded escalator, we heard someone call out, "Melinda Doolittle, of *American Idol!*"

From out of nowhere, it seemed, a sea of people suddenly

surrounded us. I was beginning to realize that *American Idol* was much bigger than I had thought! Not only were tourists from around the world in Johannesburg, but the show also aired there, creating a frenzied fan base. I might have enjoyed talking with fans, but Sophia and I had another flight to catch. Besides, I wasn't looking all that cute and fresh-faced after our eighteen-hour trip. I waved at the crowd as the security officers whisked us through the airport.

Sophia and I made our connection to Zambia and settled back for three more hours of flying. We were met by dignitaries who were facilitating Laura Bush's arrival, since she would be landing at about the same time.

I was excited about meeting the First Lady, but I have to admit, I was equally excited about being at the same hotel and hanging out with her Secret Service contingent. Since the first time I saw Jack Bauer on the TV show *24*, I've been fascinated by the guys wearing the black suits and those tiny earpieces. I had even dreamed of being an agent someday. Now here I was observing them up close!

The following morning I dressed in conservative—and protective—black slacks and a black, short-sleeved wrap-around top, with flats. The Malaria No More representatives took us to a rural Zambian community, where they had arranged for our group to observe the distribution of the bed nets to the local population. It was a moving scene, with dozens of men loading nets on their beat-up bicycles and then delivering them to people waiting in their tiny straw-hut homes. Sophia and I arrived before Mrs. Bush because I wanted to rehearse with the children's choir with whom I was scheduled to sing during the official welcoming ceremonies.

The children in the choir could not speak English, but they had learned the words of "Amazing Grace" so they could sing along with me. Their leader spoke minimal broken English and helped us communicate. Watching the beaming faces of those young children—most of them between the ages of eight and twelve—and hearing their exuberant voices touched my heart so deeply that tears streamed down my face. The children could somehow tell that my tears resulted from joy and compassion rather than sorrow, and they embraced me all the more. They sang several of their own indigenous songs for me, and I loved hearing them.

About that time, the Secret Service agents instructed us to line up: "The First Lady is coming!" I was every bit as excited as the children since I hadn't met Mrs. Bush yet. The First Lady arrived a few minutes later, wearing a casual but classy blue pantsuit. Jenna Bush, one of the Bushes' twin daughters, accompanied her, and these two gracious women made their way down the line, shaking hands and greeting each person warmly and naturally.

When they got to me, Mrs. Bush's eyes lit up, and she grabbed my hand. "Melinda! I'm so excited to see you!" Then the First Lady blew my mind. "I watched you every week and loved you!" she said. I was still reeling from the information that the President's wife was even aware of *American Idol*, much less a faithful viewer who, more specifically, had liked me, when Jenna Bush slipped up next to me and gave me a big hug. Right behind Laura and Jenna Bush came the then-First Lady of Zambia, Maureen Mwanawasa, a dynamic woman who helped lead her country's fight against AIDS and malaria. Somebody informed me that I would be traveling with the First Ladies for the remainder of the day. I was overwhelmed. There were two First Ladies, a president's daughter, and me! I kept wondering, *What am I doing here?*

A large crowd of people attended the formal ceremonies, as did CNN, the BBC, and other media outlets that were following Mrs. Bush. The African children presented some skits first demonstrating the problems of malaria and AIDS and then emphasizing the joy when a life is saved. As I watched, my emotions nearly got the best of me. These children's families had been devastated by disease, yet I was struck by their happy faces. Mrs. Bush gave an inspiring speech, telling the Zambian people that they could eradicate malaria and AIDS and that America was committed to help them. Then she introduced me to sing.

I gathered the children's choir, and we sang "Amazing Grace" a cappella. I made it through the song without tearing up, but at several points, I felt as though I were outside myself, listening to the beautiful harmonies of the Zambian children around me. I could see tears in the eyes of some people at the front of the crowd, and it was obvious that something (or Somebody!) beyond me was at work here. After the official ceremonies ended, we helped put together "Care Kits" and packed them on bikes to be delivered.

On the way back to our hotel, I learned that Mrs. Mwanawasa was hosting a formal dinner for Mrs. Bush that night and that I was invited. *Oh, no!* I thought. *I haven't packed anything to wear to such an event*—and the invitation said we were to dress in traditional African garb. Sophia, Martin, and I went shopping, and while I was exchanging my American dollars for Zambian currency, the woman at the counter looked up and said, "You were on *American Idol.*"

"How do you know that?" Martin asked.

"I know her face," she answered. We went next door to a grocery to grab some snacks before dinner, and again I heard someone gush, "Melinda Doolittle!" I couldn't believe it. There I was in a Zambian grocery store, and someone recognized me from *American Idol*. A man and a woman approached me and introduced themselves. They explained that the program aired at 3:00 a.m., but they stayed up to watch it. I was beginning to understand the far-reaching impact of being on that show, far greater than I had ever imagined.

We found a black and gold ensemble appropriate for me to wear to the formal dinner, and I hurried back to my room to get ready. At the dinner, I sat with Mrs. Bush's chief of staff and Admiral Timothy Ziemer, an American working in Zambia with Malaria No More. The state dinner was a formal but lively event, filled with surprises. The Zambian First Lady spoke passionately and eloquently about her country's efforts to defeat malaria and AIDS, and she expressed profound gratitude for America's partnership. Then it was time for some entertainment.

On a stage in the corner of the ballroom, a group performed traditional dances and songs. Then a men's vocal group sang, first in their native tongue and then in English. As I listened, I realized, *They're singing worship songs!* I guess I shouldn't have been surprised since Zambia is a former British colony and still predominantly Christian. I was thrilled at the people's freedom to express their deep faith even at a government function, a freedom we've come so close to abdicating in our own country.

The songs continued throughout the evening, and women

were often called on to join in the dancing. The Zambian representatives, in a vibrant rainbow of traditional dresses, eagerly took the floor. At one point, Mrs. Mwanawasa joined in, as did Carmen Martinez, the American ambassador to Zambia. The Zambians dedicated a song to Mrs. Bush and asked her to join them in singing it. The First Lady graciously agreed and stepped onto the stage. Unbeknownst to her, the song the Zambians had learned in English was from *Mary Poppins*, and, although "A Spoonful of Sugar (Makes the Medicine Go Down)" might have been more appropriate, the Zambians asked the First Lady to join them in "Supercalifragilisticexpialidocious"! I couldn't wait to see what Mrs. Bush was going to do with that one. But without a bit of hesitation, Mrs. Bush joined in, singing and dancing right along with the Zambians. I watched in amazement, thinking, *I love this woman! As distinguished as she is, she's not afraid to be herself.* Later, Mrs. Bush joked that although she couldn't quite match the moves of Mrs. Mwanawasa, she at least beat Jenna onto the dance floor!

Following their performance, one of the aides came to our table and whispered, "The First Ladies would like you to sing the song you sang earlier today." A jolt of fear shot through my system, but how could I possibly refuse such a request! Without any rehearsing, I stepped onto the platform and, along with the Zambian group, sang two hymns, one of which was "Amazing Grace." The audience seemed deeply moved.

I learned so much about the Zambian people and their relationship with the U.S. on my brief trip. Interestingly, the people of Africa held President Bush in much higher regard than many people did in our home country. In Africa, he was a hero for leading the fight against AIDS and malaria, something I hadn't realized before traveling to Africa and seeing the results of his efforts.

The next day I visited more children in Zambian hospitals and clinics as well as a class of pregnant women learning how to use the bed nets properly. When I asked medical workers what they most needed, I expected them to request more medical supplies. Imagine my surprise when they said, "We need clean water"—and that was in the clinics! We take so much for granted in our nation. The entire trip to Africa was an eye-opening and heart-expanding experience for me, and I will never be the same. Never again will I base my joy on what I have, but I will be thankful for every blessing in my life.

When I returned to America, I could hardly contain my excitement about having gone to Africa, and I was even more motivated to help meet the many needs I had seen.

Most of us feel that because we can't do something "big," it isn't worth doing anything at all, but that simply is not true. A mere ten dollars can provide a bed net that can save the lives of up to four children in Africa. Making a difference in the life of even one of God's precious children really does matter.

My fan club, called Melinda's Backups™, has since taken up the challenge to help fight malaria and has continued to raise money to provide bed nets. While I was on the *American Idol* tour, not only did the fan club send flowers to every venue, but they also donated bed nets for every show I did. Even now, the Backups have come up with numerous ways to raise thousands of dollars for Malaria No More, including running in the Country Music Marathon every year. These remarkable fans are truly making a difference!

When you look for some way to make a difference, don't worry that you cannot touch the entire world. Simply look for a way that you can touch one person. God can touch the world, and He will start through you. And there's an extra blessing! As you get involved in helping meet the needs of helpless, hurting people, God will meet your needs in ways you cannot even imagine!

5

On Time Is Soon Enough

The first time I heard my mom say, "On time is soon enough," I didn't get what the big deal was. The statement seemed like a no-brainer. If a professor said a paper was due on Monday, as long as I turned it in by then, it was soon enough. However, Mom's statement went much deeper than that. She was referring to God's timing. For instance, I could pray and ask God for something that I felt like I needed immediately. If I didn't get it right at that moment, I got upset. Then a few days later, when I did receive His answer to that prayer, it turned out to be the most perfect timing in the world. On time was soon enough.

When I was about nine years old, I started asking for a puppy.

"We'll get one when the time is right," Mom promised. I'm pretty sure she added, "On time is soon enough." Of course I didn't want to hear that!

The following year we moved to Tulsa, and the apartment my mom chose was very pet friendly. Soon after our move, a wonderful family named the Gunters gave us a gorgeous toy poodle that I promptly fell in love with and named Cuddles. She was the perfect dog . . . in the perfect place . . . at—gulp—the *perfect* time.

After graduating from college, while I was still in the transition period between getting a diploma and trying to make a living in the Nashville music community, I relied heavily on Mom for emotional and spiritual support, and on occasion I relied on her financially. One month my rent was coming due, and I knew that I didn't have enough money to pay it. I called Mom and asked for her assistance.

"This is the hardest thing Mommy has to do, but I can't help you this time," she said. "God is your Source; nobody else. You have to learn to trust God to provide for you."

"But, Mom, my rent is due next week. What am I supposed to do? I'm running out of time."

"On time is soon enough, Melinda."

This was definitely *not* a time I wanted to hear those words!

I prayed that somehow God would provide a way for me to pay my rent, which was due on the first of the month. But the first came, and I still did not have enough money to pay the bill. My rent was not considered past due until the fifth of the month, so I still had hope as I tried to scrape up every available penny. The second and third days passed, and still I was short. On the fourth of the month, I went to my mailbox, and inside it was an envelope. I tore it open and found a check that had come as payment for a background session I had almost forgotten. The check provided just enough for me to pay my rent before it was late.

When I called to tell Mom the good news, she said, "See, baby, God will provide. The answer may not come when you think it should, but on time is soon enough."

As much as I didn't want to hear that quote again, I knew in that moment that it was absolutely true.

Not long ago, a friend of mine was going through a difficult period. She and her husband were trying to have a baby, and it wasn't happening as quickly as she wanted. Without even thinking, I said gently, "On time is soon enough." My initial reaction was *Oh, no! I'm sounding like my mother!* But then I thought to myself, *And that is a pretty good thing.*

Good Versus the Best

I'm convinced that the toughest choices in life are not always about good versus evil, but good versus the best. Sometimes we have to say no to something good so we can say yes to something better, and that often ends up being the best for our lives. Knowing that God has your best interests at heart helps ease the pain when you turn down something good in hopes that He has something better in mind for you. But that doesn't always make it easy.

On my way back from Africa, my booking agent at the time had set up an audition for me in New York the very day I returned to the U.S. The audition was for a part in a Broadway musical, but the part for which I was asked to audition was not a role I wanted to play. I told my agent that he probably shouldn't even have submitted my name to try out, but he thought that once I auditioned, I might change my mind if I were offered the part. I had done some theater in local productions and very much hoped to earn a spot in a Broadway show one day, so to audition was indeed an honor. But the particular role for which the agent was promoting me had some content that I found objectionable.

Nevertheless, I did the audition as he requested, and that's when things got even more interesting. Amazingly, I was offered a lead role right on the spot. Ordinarily, producers like to take some time to consider their options after the auditions, so I wasn't really expecting to hear anything for several weeks. Instead, the director said to me that very day, "We'll be contacting your agent, but the part is yours."

Now I really had a dilemma. I didn't want to disappoint the agency that had expressed such confidence in me, nor did I want to disappoint the producers and the director of the Broadway show. To be selected for such a part was like a dream come true. But, deep inside, I knew the role was not for me.

I called my pastor and talked through the decision with him. In my heart and mind, I had already built my case as to why I should not accept the role, and I was hoping he might confirm what I was feeling. After listening carefully and asking a few questions, my pastor said, "I'm in total agreement. I think you are making the right decision."

I could hear my mom's voice in my mind as well. Mom always says, "When making decisions, even if the circumstances look like you should go a certain direction, but you believe God wants you to go a different way, you should do what causes you to have peace in your heart and mind. If you know, go with what you know."

I knew in my heart what I had to do. And once I know what I'm supposed to do, my mind is set.

I turned down the part.

Not surprisingly, my booking agent was not pleased. He applied even more pressure.

"I understand why you want me to do the show," I said, "but this isn't the one for me."

The agent was adamant that I should take the part and promised to call me back.

Over the next few days, I was on an emotional roller coaster as I tried to get back into the *Idol* rehearsal routine and put Broadway out of my mind. I went on to Florida to catch up with my fellow *Idol* cast members, and we opened our show two days later. About a week into the show, I received a phone call backstage at the arena. On the line were my agent, the director of the Broadway show, and one of the major financiers of the show. They all urged me to take the part, and, as kindly as I could, I attempted to explain that I didn't feel it was the right role for me.

Round and round the conversation went, and the tension seemed almost palpable. I didn't even want to think about how angry my agent was getting. But when they heard the resolution in my voice, the financier said, "There are a lot of things that I said no to when others thought I should say yes. But that's one of the reasons I am where I am today."

That settled the issue. The conversation ended on a positive note; unfortunately, my involvement with the agent did not. My decision to turn down the role on Broadway cost me a lot in terms of that particular relationship, but it was the right decision for me. It also turned out to be a good business decision, since the show closed unexpectedly after a brief run. I could never have imagined that, but God knew ahead of time and guided my steps in a different direction.

Saying no to something good when a better opportunity is not on the horizon is scary, especially when you don't have a safe place to fall back to or a security blanket to hold on to. When I turned down the Broadway show, I had no idea what was going to happen after the *American Idol* tour was complete or how I was going to make a living.

But within a short time, I was in negotiations for a recording deal. I had previously sung background for a number of artists, both gospel and mainstream. During that time, it became one of my dreams to inspire audiences that might not ordinarily listen to a gospel artist, so as I considered record labels, I kept that in mind. I wanted to align myself with someone who understood my heart and what I wanted to do with my music.

I finally found the perfect recording company for me: Hi Fi Recordings, a smaller, independent label in New York. This would be my first solo recording. It was a whole new adventure!

John Titta, the label's resident song genius, came to Nashville with some songs that he had handpicked just for me.

As soon as I heard them, I instantly connected with the material. Songs such as Aretha Franklin's "Wonderful," the gorgeous ballad "If I'm Not in Love with You," and others all struck perfect chords with me. Hi Fi connected me with an amazing producer, Mike Mangini, who took the songs I loved and created wonderful retro-soul tracks that immediately made me excited to sing. I did the majority of my vocals in New York, and I started the recording process where I was comfortable: with the background vocals. It made it easier for me to get into the groove of the lead vocals. I was happy because the songs were eminently singable, and with their beautiful melodies and live instruments, they reminded me of songs from long ago. What an incredible thrill to complete my first album, not as a background singer, but as a new artist!

We released the album *Coming Back to You* in February 2009, and it received wonderful reviews. It was a tremendous first effort, and I was ecstatic.

Had I done the Broadway show when it was offered, I might never have been able to record that album and work with those incredible musicians and label executives.

I know that someday I'm going to get a chance to fulfill my dream of being on Broadway, but it will be at the right time . . . with the right people . . . in the perfect show for me. On time is soon enough.

6

Chew the Hay and Spit Out the Sticks

From the time I was a little girl, Mom taught me to "chew the hay and spit out the sticks." In other words, you can't allow criticism or negative statements of any kind to get you down. When somebody criticizes you, if there is anything helpful or if there is any kernel of truth in the criticism, take what is good and spit out the rest.

My mom is an amazing teacher. Over the years, Mom taught every grade from elementary school to high school and also worked in administration, but her forte was teaching special-needs children. She has an extraordinary heart of compassion. Often her students would get taunted for being in special classes, and because of their unique needs, they were reminded every day that they were learning disabled, or LD.

But Mom took a different tack. "LD doesn't stand for learning disabled," Mom taught her students. "It stands for 'Learning Differently.'" To watch her students take those words to heart was so wonderful. Because Mom taught her LD students the simple lesson of how to turn criticism around, their lives were changed. They walked taller, they acted more confidently, and they started to fit in more easily with their peers. It was tremendously fulfilling for Mom when one of her students returned to a regular classroom and functioned right alongside the other children.

She was teaching them to chew the hay and spit out the sticks.

Dealing with Criticism

I try to find the humor in criticism, if possible, and I don't want to take things so seriously that I'm afraid to laugh at myself. Mom always said, "You might as well laugh. If you don't laugh, other people are going to."

After the first *Idol* broadcast I appeared on, the Internet bloggers were downright cruel, saying that I looked like a boll weevil. I called home and lamented, "Mom, they're saying that I look like a boll weevil!"

"A boll weevil? Isn't that a bug?" Mom asked. She went online and found a picture of a boll weevil. A few seconds later, I heard her cracking up with laughter. "Well, maybe just a little bit," she said.

"MOM!"

Other bloggers complained that I had no neck. "How can she even sing without a neck?" they asked. "She looks like Shrek!" The name stuck, and I was called Shrek on a daily basis. One comedy bit said that I would be great for a Head and Shoulders shampoo commercial because I had no neck. For most of the *American Idol* competition, I was called "no-neck Shrek."

TMZ, the gossip website, superimposed a picture of my face onto Shrek's. At first I didn't think it was all that funny, but I've learned to laugh about it. I even used the photo online during Halloween.

Handling criticism is never easy, but it's even tougher to take when it is unmerited or comes from people who do not have expertise on the subject or credibility you can respect. Anyone can have an opinion, but not everyone's opinion is valid or accurate.

As a contestant on *American Idol*, you can't help but deal with criticism. The main point of the show is for you to be judged.

Each of the contestants in my season handled it differently, and I learned from each of them. Season six was Gina Glocksen's third time to audition for *American Idol*. Even though the judges had sent her home in previous years, she was determined to go after her dream, and she kept coming back. Her perseverance paid off, and she not only made it to the show, but she made it all the way to ninth place during our season.

Lakisha Jones is a go-getter. She doesn't stop until she gets what she wants. Her drive was so impressive to me. No matter what people around her said or did, she remained focused on her goal. Lakisha, too, was a Top 10 finalist on *Idol*.

Phil Stacey, another finalist, turned to his family for support, and it was so incredible to see his strong faith and foundation be a comfort for him.

Surprisingly, I learned the most from Sanjaya Malakar, the most controversial contestant of the season. Sanjaya was like the little brother I never wanted. So young and full of energy, he would run around backstage and do things like lick our faces or jump on us for a piggyback ride down the hall. It was all too common to hear one of us yelling, "SANJAYA! STOP!"

But for all his youthful enthusiasm, I absolutely adored the big-hearted, slim-framed boy with hair that made us all jealous. The more I watched him, the more I learned. Every day there were awful statements in the media about Sanjaya. Most of the things said about him would have broken me in a minute, but not him. He was resilient. When critics spoke or wrote negatively about his voice, he just practiced harder. He truly has a beautiful voice, as evidenced by his tender performance of "Besame Mucho." The media, unfortunately, never gave him a break. Sanjaya's ability to remain undaunted and not let the harsh words affect him spoke volumes to me. I was so impressed by the way he handled himself, by his capacity to chew the hay and spit out the sticks.

The scorpion-like stings of criticism sink even more deeply under our skin when the intent is clearly cruel. Long after *Idol's* Season Six was over, I saw a blog by a former *Idol* cast member that put down almost every contestant and belittled everything about me, from my singing to my album sales. I knew I shouldn't have read it in the first place, but once I let my eyes fall on those harsh words, I was hooked. I couldn't stop reading until I had ingested every word, and by that time I was fuming in anger.

The person who wrote the blog had never been one of my favorites. You probably know this kind of person, the kind about whom I have been known to say, "I don't like you. I love you because Jesus says I have to, but He doesn't say I have to like you. And I don't!"

Suddenly, in the recesses of my mind, I heard my mother's voice saying, "Don't let this ruin things for you. You still have to walk in forgiveness. If you remain angry at the person who offended you, it doesn't do that person any good or harm, but it affects you."

I knew in an instant that I had to forgive the writer. I can't say that it was easy; and I certainly didn't want to, but I began to say aloud, "I forgive the person who said these things. I forgive this person who so callously hurt me. I don't need to defend myself. And every time this person says something else, I'll keep forgiving. My actions will prove him wrong." I kept saying it until I actually believed it, and then I knew I had indeed forgiven. It's not always easy to do the right thing, but it is always worth it.

One of the people who gave me some great advice regarding criticism was Ellen DeGeneres. I had the honor of meeting Ellen during the "Idol Gives Back" episodes. She took time out to speak with me about the road ahead. She cautioned me that I would see a lot of things about myself online and in print, most of them good, but some of them hurtful. Then she said, "After all the good you read about yourself, it's the one bad or hurtful comment that will stick with you the longest." She continued, "I would tell you not to look at anything written about yourself, but I know that's impossible, so you have to decide how you are going to handle the criticism." Ellen gave me tips on how to keep the put-downs in perspective. Most importantly, she reminded me that the people criticizing me had never met me, so their words were just opinions. How I let their words affect me, however, was my choice.

I appreciated Ellen's insights and thanked her for them. It meant so much to hear these words from someone who has experienced her fair share of criticism. I still use what she taught me, and I will never forget it.

And one of Ellen's observations rings especially true for me. Isn't it amazing how much credence we willingly give to criticism? I may read or hear ten wonderful things about myself, but the single bad comment is the one that sticks in my mind. It burrows deep down into my brain, all the way into my heart. To be in the public eye nowadays invites criticism, and we are bound to experience it, but we do not need to accept it as true. Even if you aren't a public person, you may receive unmerited criticism from your boss, a teacher, or a family member. Consider it and then move on. But don't dwell on it—and don't base your self-worth on conditional or transitory factors such as what someone says about you, how you look, how well you perform, or how popular you are in the eyes of the world.

When you are criticized, search for something constructive in the harsh words. Take that good, make any positive changes possible, and let the bad stuff roll right off you. Or, as my mom taught me, chew the hay and spit out the sticks.

7

Know Your Worth

Know Your Worth in Relationships

My record for dating is a perfect 0–7. Therefore I feel fully qualified to tell you what not to do when it comes to relationships. Here are a few lessons I've learned along the way.

Don't base your self-worth on whether or not you have a significant other.

I was never known as the pretty girl. I have always been awkward, clumsy, and more of a tomboy. The only time I have felt pretty or worth something was when a guy noticed me. That meant every time I wasn't noticed, which was the majority of the time, I felt awful—and awful about myself. I finally realized that I was created perfectly, and whether or not guys noticed, there was beauty in just knowing that fact.

One year in high school, I didn't have a date to the prom. But a group of special-needs students at our high school had won a contest, and the prize was limousine transportation to the prom. At first the girls didn't want to go, but I said, "Of course you should go. All five of you can go as my dates!"

We went to the prom together, and we took a few homeschooled students as well, girls who might not have been able to attend the prom otherwise. We dressed up in evening gowns, and Mom bought us corsages. No doubt, we made for an odd spectacle on the dance floor, with all of us girls out there—several in wheelchairs—dancing together. But we had the best time!

Don't get into a relationship just because the person fills one need in your life.

When I'm scared, when I'm walking into something unknown, I look for security. In the past, if there was a man around who offered safety and security, I would simply jump into the relationship without even checking to see if he had any of the other qualities I was looking for. That's a recipe for disaster.

Don't assume the person will change.

This is the most common issue I deal with personally, and it is also the issue I hear most about from young women I meet. We get excited just because someone likes us, and we think we can make his temper better or make him treat us differently once he starts dating us. But it's not fair to expect him to change, and it's definitely not cool to try to manipulate him into changing.

Be the good thing.

I remember hearing my pastor's wife talk about a verse in the Bible that says a man who finds a wife finds a good thing. She explained to the women in the room that our course of action was just to "be the good thing." Her advice really made me think. I had determined that I was looking for a Cliff Huxtable. I wanted someone who thought outside the box, who always made me laugh and smile, someone who made love fun. I had even written these qualities in a special notebook. However, after hearing the pastor's wife say those words, I decided to make a new list—for myself. What kind of woman do I need to be to deserve a Cliff? Naturally, I need to be Claire: levelheaded, successful, and able to drop my guard at a moment's notice and just have fun. Suffice it to say, I'm still working on those things.

I have a fabulous example of a true man in my dad. He is such a caring and loving gentleman. He's a constant reminder that wonderful men are out there and that they are so worth the wait.

Know Your Worth on the Job

After a few years of trying to establish myself in the Nashville music scene, I was working steadily as a studio background singer. That was the good news; the bad news was that I wasn't always getting paid. At the beginning of my career, I tried to sing as often as I could, and that meant that I would frequently take jobs that didn't pay. After a while, however, my lack of income was less about establishing myself as a singer and more about not feeling as though I was worth a paycheck.

"What do you charge to sing?" someone might ask.

"Oh, just whatever you feel comfortable with," I'd respond. Actually, my payment had nothing to do with someone else's comfort level. I was the one who wasn't comfortable asking for a specific amount. What would I do, I fretted, if they said, "You're not worth that much"?

My roommate at the time, Stacey Merida, had worked in the music business for a number of years. She knew I was working all the time, but she also knew that I sometimes had trouble paying my share of the rent. So one day she sat me down and said, "Melinda, do you know what you are worth? Do you have any idea what it means for you to go on the road with someone as a singer or to work in the studio? Can you put a price tag on your time and talents?"

"But I don't want to charge anyone too much to have me sing," I protested.

"I understand that," Stacey said, "but it's important to know what you are worth. Singing is not simply a hobby for you; it is your craft, it's your profession, and you work hard at it. If someone can't afford the fee for your services, you can always negotiate, but you need to be able to make a living, to go out on the road or sing in the studio and earn enough money to have a home to come back to. Take some time to think through the services you provide as a singer and the value of those services."

I took Stacey's advice and thought about the different things I brought to the table when someone hired me as a background singer. I also talked with professionals in the music industry, including producers, artists, and other background singers with whom I regularly worked. I came up with what I thought was a reasonable fee for my services compared to others who were doing something similar. When I first began charging a fee for my singing, nobody ever said, "No, we can't do that," or "Oh, I'm sorry, that's out of our budget." The people who employed me knew that I would work hard for them, that I would come prepared to do the best job possible, and that I would give them more than their money's worth.

Believe in Yourself

I had the privilege of singing with some extraordinary artists during my time as a background singer. One who made a significant impact on me is the legendary Sheila E., a Grammy-nominated artist best known for her collaborations with Prince. She has had several number one hits and has been a pioneer for women in the music industry.

There were ten of us singing background on the "Sisters in the Spirit" tour for a roster of incredible artists, including Yolanda Adams, Kelly Price, Martha Munizzi, RiZen, and Juanita Bynum. Sheila E. was the musical director, and she and I hit it off immediately.

On one song Sheila featured her background singers, asking three of us each night to sing a solo ad-lib section at the end. A few days into the tour, Sheila said to me, "Let's keep alternating the three solos, but I want you to sing a solo every night."

"Oh no!" I answered. "I'm not here to sing lead. Please ask one of the other singers. I'm sure one of them will do a much better job than I would."

Sheila knew when she offered me the solo that I was reluctant to sing by myself. She smiled and said, "It's that attitude that made me want to give you the part in the first place. But I don't want to put you in a position that makes you uncomfortable." I was so grateful that she didn't pressure me to step out when I wasn't ready. After that, Sheila spent a great deal of time pouring her heart into me.

By the end of the tour, I still had not done a solo. Even though we were supposed to alternate the three solo sections at the end of that song, I managed to pass along my turn every time it came up. Finally, on the last night of the tour, Sheila came to me and said, "I'm not angry that you haven't taken a solo, but I want you to know that I noticed."

Near the close of the show, as usual, Sheila featured the background singers. She went right down the line, nodding to each vocalist to do a short vamp. When she came to me, I shook my head no, so Sheila went on to the next person in line. *Whew*, I thought. *I made it through the tour.* But just then Sheila stepped up and, while the band was still vamping, walked over to me and said, "Now, ladies and gentlemen, I have a treat for you. This young lady has not sung a solo the entire tour, but you are going to get to hear her tonight. Tonight is her night to step out. So, Melinda, take my microphone and come on out here." She pointed to center stage.

I was petrified with fear! I'm sure I gave Sheila a horrified look as she handed me the microphone. But what could I do? I stepped up and started singing, and the band followed right along with me. Before I knew it, I was getting into it. The band really got into it, too, and after the initial nausea, I had the time of my life! We went on for about two minutes, and when I was done, the audience was cheering and applauding wildly—and both Sheila and I were boo-hooing.

After the concert, I raced to Sheila's dressing room and literally tackled her! "What were you thinking?" I stammered.

Sheila laughed and said, "But you had fun, didn't you?"

I hugged her like I was never going to let go. "Yes, I did," I confessed. "I loved it!" I had to admit that Sheila's encouragement had pushed me out of my comfort zone. "But you still scared the living daylights out of me!"

"Sometimes that's the way it has to happen," Sheila said. "Melinda, I believe in you. You just have to believe in yourself." That night I realized that my disbelief really did affect the people around me. I vowed to start believing in myself. It's a conscious decision that I now choose to make every day, and so should you. You're worth it!

Keeping Yourself Real

One of the best ways to stay real is to keep some people around you who know you well, people who will help keep your feet on the ground and your head out of the clouds. My closest friends and family members know me for who I am, and they loved me long before *American Idol*—and they have loved me since then. They aren't "yes people," so they are not bashful about telling me what they really think. They don't look at me as "Melinda Doolittle, Musical Package or Product"; they know me simply as Melinda.

My dad is now married to Harriet, whom we affectionately call MiMi. Exceptionally bright and witty—and the perfect woman for my father—she is also a classic example of keeping it real. No matter what, I know she will always give me her honest opinion, and give it with tact and humor. Her daughter, Pam, is the sister I've always wanted, and, like her mom, she never lets me get away with anything. At our family get-togethers, we now have a tradition of "girl talk," and we talk straightforwardly about guys, work, and frustrations. MiMi and Pam are not bashful about prodding, probing, and offering their suggestions about circumstances in my life. Their input is invaluable to me, and I love them for it! They help keep me real.

Girls Just Want to Have Fun

I don't get to entertain a lot, mainly because I travel so much, but I have been able to continue the tradition of "girls' night" that my mom started with me. I try to act like a big sister to some young girls I know and pass on some of the wisdom I have gained through trial and error. They openly share with me some of the issues they are dealing with—peer pressure, sexual pressures, school pressures, conflicts with their parents, and so much more. I sometimes scare myself, though, because I hear myself sounding so much like my mother when I offer advice to the girls.

Normally when that happens, the girls reply, "Oh, Melinda, that's what my mom says too."

I can't help but smile.

Sometimes these young women just need to hear an outside voice echoing many of the same things they hear from their parents.

We also talk about clothing and being modest, which is not always easy with today's fashions. I encountered that problem every week on *American Idol*. The show gave every contestant a stipend to go out and purchase some stage clothes for each night of competition. Along with a wardrobe stylist from *Idol*, I'd hit the mall each week searching for something stylish. But I did not want to wear anything too tight, nor did I want to show a lot of skin. It was tough to find show clothing in which I would feel comfortable, and I had more than a few "discussions" with the stylists assigned to me.

One of them summed up our dilemma when he explained, "We can find you something you look good in, or we can find you something you like."

But I truly believe that it *is* possible to dress stylishly yet modestly. It takes some effort and creativity, but it can be done, and I let the girls who stay overnight in my home know that it is okay to go against the grain, to be a nonconformist in a positive way. I tell them, "It shows how strong you are and how independent you are when you have the courage to buck the norm by covering up more skin rather than exposing yourself. Always remember that you are valuable."

When I tell them that I wasn't allowed to date until I was sixteen, the girls' eyes widen in surprise, but I can tell that it makes them feel better about their own parents who might have similar rules. "There are lots of great guys out there, and you will have plenty of time to date," I tell the girls. "But right now just find out who you are and don't allow someone else to dictate how you feel about yourself."

My *favorite* thing to teach the girls is how to lose well, something I learned over and over again from my mother. I well remember my first lesson in losing graciously. My mom annihilated me at Connect Four, and she reminded me that it was my responsibility to congratulate her. I was only about five years of age and hadn't yet learned how to control my emotions. Through heaving breaths, I sobbed, "I'm so happy for you, Mommy!"

I have a room in my house known as the Wii Room where the girls and I play all sorts of games. I never *let* them win. And when I win, I remind them, "It is important that you learn how to lose graciously and to be happy for others when they win, especially if it's me!"

I particularly love to play Wii with my niece Kalyn. She's just as competitive as I am, so it makes it even better when I beat her!

I like letting the competitive part of me come out to play, and one of the best ways for me to do that is by playing air hockey. I *love* air hockey! In fact, the highlight of my fan club get-togethers is the air hockey challenge, in which I play members of Melinda's Backups™. Sometimes I will play against as many as twelve to fifteen players in an evening. I don't go easy on them either. I play to win, and I usually do. Just as my mom taught me, I feel called to help them learn how to lose graciously! One of the members of the fan club is blind, so I did feel bad for a few moments when I beat her, but she got me back and whipped me good.

"How did you beat me?" I whined.

"I can hear where the puck is going," she told me. "Do you mean you can't hear that?"

"No, you have supersonic hearing; I don't," I said. "And that's cheating!" Technically, she beat me fair and square, and she never lets me forget it.

Chucking the Comparisons

One of the most important things you can ever learn is to appreciate who you are. Other people may try to pigeonhole you or force you into their preconceived notions of who or what you should be, but God created you to be unique.

Sometimes in the media I get compared to other singers. Of course, at times it is extremely flattering to see my name in the same sentence with Gladys Knight, Aretha Franklin, or Tina Turner. Certainly, I'm beyond honored to be compared to these great female artists. Yet if I were to take those press reports seriously, those statements could produce enormous, unnecessary pressure and take my focus away from who I'm really supposed to be.

I can't step onto a stage thinking, *The audience is expecting Aretha Franklin and Gladys Knight to walk out there—with a side of Tina Turner thrown in for good measure.* They're going to get Melinda. When I perform, I can only be myself. Of course I respect every one of those amazing singers and have learned so much from each of them, but I can only be Melinda.

Obviously, we live in a world of constant comparisons, and many of us work in extremely competitive environments. It is always tempting to allow comparisons to other people to dictate how we will look, act, speak, or even think. We can't escape comparisons—*American Idol* is comparison to the max—but we don't have to let those comparisons change our core values.

It's easy for people to base their worth on what others say about them; they use the opinions of other people as a barometer to gauge how well they are doing. But that gauge is unreliable and sometimes even dangerous. When I find myself falling into that trap, I love to look at one of my favorite Scripture passages, from Psalm 139:

> For you created my inmost being;
>   you knit me together in my mother's womb.
> I praise you because I am fearfully and wonderfully made;
>   your works are wonderful,
>   I know that full well.
> My frame was not hidden from you
>   when I was made in the secret place.
>   When I was woven together in the depths of the earth,
> your eyes saw my unformed body.
>   All the days ordained for me
>   were written in your book
>   before one of them came to be. (Psalm 139:13–16 NIV)

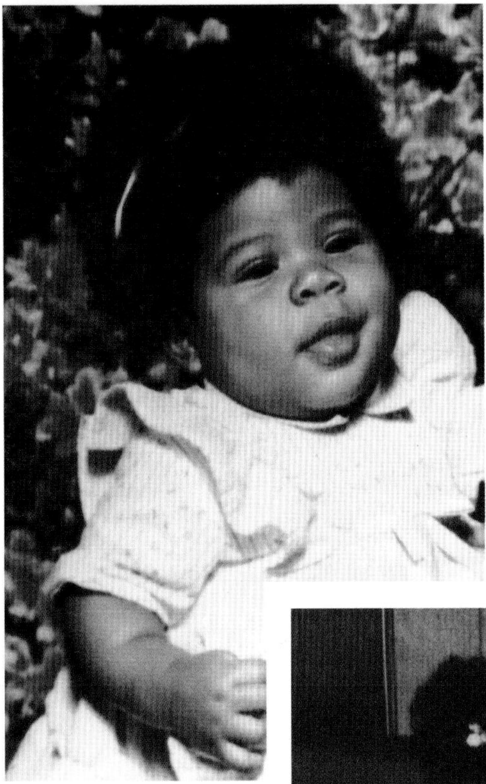

After all these years, my hair hasn't changed. :)

Chilling at my Daddy's house. I was so cool. →

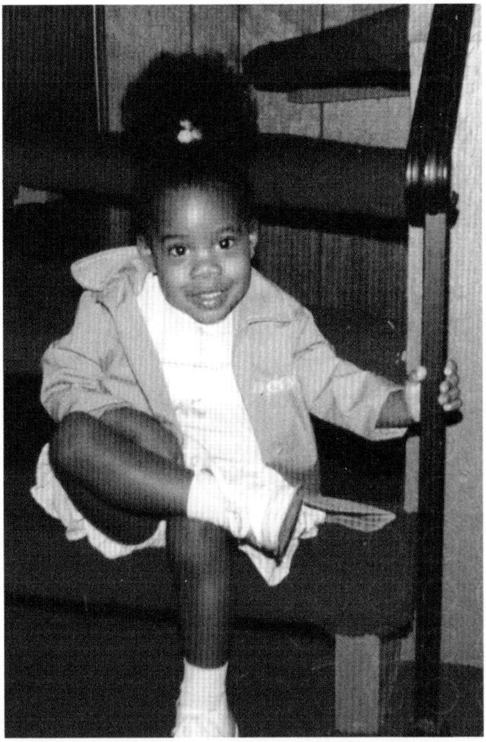

My family!

L-R: Harriett aka Mi-Mi, Me, Daddy, Kalyn and Pam.

← Me and my gorgeous Mommy!

I was the mascot at Union High School. We were the RedSkins and this was my costume... Seriously! →

I really like pie!

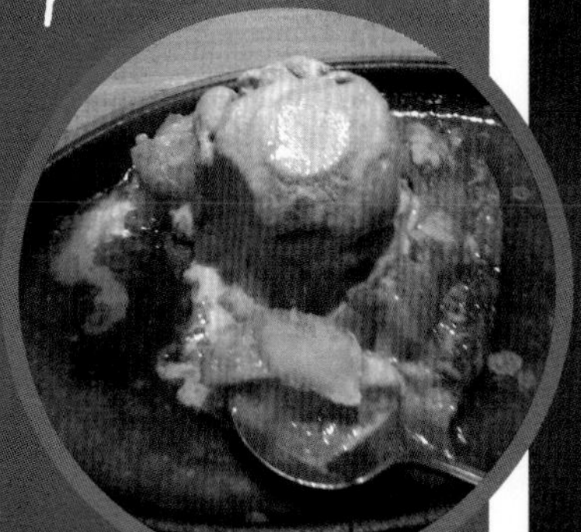

Jon Bon Jovi -
I'm a rocker!

Shrek the Third

Janet, Kelley and I before my flight to American Idol.

Me and my baby girl, Jordin!

Flowers from the Backups!

Janet, Kelly and Amy - I have background singers - yay!

ONE
Bono, teaching us to make a difference. Peace!

My two Moms and my Dad, wearing their required wardrobe. :-)

Speaking to kids about Dreaming Big!

Visiting a school with the LEAGUE.

Mommy and I at the Ronald McDonald House in Nashville. I'm Scared of clowns...

At Born Again Church with Pastor Hockett during my Idol visit home Love my Pastor!

The Boys and Girls Club in Connecticut

My inner child comes out often: ATV ride in Cozumel.

Disney World! (I'm a princess)

The amazing Children's Choir in Zambia. Am I short?

Meeting more gorgeous children in Zambia.

I'm an African drummer!

My new friend in Tanzania with her very 1st Swizzler.

My bed net in Africa.

Going to the races for Malaria No More... we won!

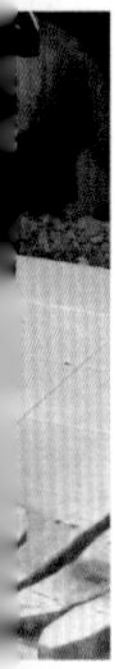

The Tanzania Delegates and the Air Force Jet. So cool!

I always wanted to be in the Secret Service. They even let me wear their sunglasses. Look out, Jack Bauer

First Lady Laura Bush introduced me before I sang. ↑

Dinner at the White House - seated right next to the President... WOW!!! →

In the studio recording my debut CD.

My CD! I'm seriously on a street in NY, dodging cars. I look calm because I'm a professional. LOL! :)

To me, that passage says that we matter to God: He made us, and even before we were born, He established a plan for our lives. We cannot base our estimation of ourselves on the fickle opinions of other people.

That's why I believe I am only in competition with myself. Certainly, I want to be the best "me" possible, so I work at my craft. I try to take good care of my body, mind, and spirit. But I don't base my self-esteem on someone else's idea of who I should be. Funny, many of the images of celebrities or models in magazines nowadays are "computer enhanced," altered to look better by someone who is handy with a mouse. The images themselves are not even real, much less valid comparisons.

So rather than comparing yourself to anyone else, simply relax and enjoy being the person God made you to be. You are your own competition. In fact, you are your only competition.

Accepting Imperfection

We should never accept mediocrity, but the sooner we realize that imperfections are normal and okay, the healthier we will be. I can be too hard on myself at times—and sometimes I'm not hard enough!

When it comes to food and maintaining my weight, for

instance, I can go to extremes. I can tell myself, "Okay, you can only eat salads and fruit and maybe a couple of nuts. That's all you get." But that routine lasts only for about two days. I just can't stand dieting. It isn't even practical for me because I'm on the road so much. On the other hand, at times I'll go to the opposite extreme and eat anything I want, and that isn't wise either. I've tried to find a healthy balance by taking care of myself. We come in various sizes and shapes, and I'm comfortable with the truth that I don't have to fit into a size two dress.

I've had a hard time with conventional beauty. I didn't get asked out on a lot of dates in high school or college. I was the "fun girl," the best friend, rather than the woman all the guys wanted to date. Eventually, when I did start dating, I found it hard to believe these guys really found me attractive.

It's taken a long time—and I'm not fully there yet—to realize that there is a beauty within me that others can see even when I cannot. I love how the Scripture says it:

> Don't be concerned about the outward beauty of fancy hairstyles, expensive jewelry, or beautiful clothes. You should clothe yourselves instead with the beauty that comes from within, the unfading beauty of a gentle and quiet spirit, which is so precious to God. (1 Peter 3:3–4 NLT)

External beauty is fragile; it can be gone in a moment. But the beauty that comes from knowing your worth doesn't depend on other people or superficial trappings. One of my favorite songs is "Imagine Me" by Kirk Franklin.

Imagine me
Loving what I see when the mirror looks at me cause I
I imagine me
In a place of no insecurities
And I'm finally happy cause
I imagine me
Imagine me, being free, trusting you totally finally I can . . .
Imagine me
I admit it was hard to see
You being in love with someone like me
But finally I can . . .
Imagine me.[1]

These lyrics help me remember that God created me beautiful—inside and out. That said, being an artist makes many image-driven demands on me. I remember when someone from my recording label said, "You're gaining a

1. "Imagine Me." Words and music by Kirk Franklin. © 2005 Zomba Songs/Kerrion Publishing (adm. by Zomba Songs/LillyMack Music [BMI]). Used by permission.

little weight, Melinda." Ooh, that was rough! That person was right: I was gaining weight—because I like pie! But I didn't want to hear that. I went home and cried. I cried until I got the hurt out of my system, and then I decided to do something about it.

My best motivation is often to prove somebody wrong. Case in point: I once received an offer to be on a television weight-loss program. Now that's an offer you don't want to get. For them to even offer meant that they saw me as someone who needed to lose weight. That got me thinking, *I need to get back in shape so they won't ever consider asking me to be on that show again.* Television adds at least ten pounds to a person, so when I'd see myself on various shows, I'd cringe. *Okay, time to go back on the healthy eating plan and start exercising again.* I bought an exercise machine and put it right next to my bed, where it would be the first thing I saw every day. If I had put it in another location, I could have found some excuse to avoid it, but with the machine staring at me each morning as soon as I opened my eyes, I was forced to confront it. I knew I needed to exercise, and I don't really care for gyms, so the home exercise unit really helped me.

I did find one program where I was comfortable exercising with other people. My friend Mandisa introduced me to

Zumba, a hip-hop, Latin aerobics class. I fell in love with it the first day, and I can't get enough, which is good, since I can't get enough pie either.

Good Hair

Another source of insecurity for me has often been my hair. While on *American Idol*, I started wearing wigs so I didn't have to deal with it at all. A couple of years after the show, I finally got to the place where I wanted to experiment with my own hair. Society may say that long, straight, flowing hair is the essence of beauty, but I beg to differ. I love my curly and often unruly hair!

An Invaluable Reflection

Knowing what you are worth, however, involves much more than appearance, talent, skills, or money. It involves understanding that you are wonderfully made in God's image, that in some profound way you are a positive reflection of Him.

I meet many young women these days who tell me their stories, and I have recognized a pattern in them. A couple of years ago, I performed at a charity event and met two young women who were volunteering there. When they sought me out to tell me how much they loved the way *American Idol* makes dreams come true, I asked—as I often do—what their dreams were. They told me that their families didn't think they'd amount to much, and they had heard this so much growing up that they had started to believe it. As I listened to their stories, something rose up within me. I said, "You have to know your worth. You can't let anyone determine that for you!"

I talked with them for an hour or more, and to this day, I still get letters from those young women saying, "Now I know my worth, and nothing can hold me back."

Knowing your worth is life changing. It is a daily choice—sometimes a minute-by-minute choice—that can produce a quiet strength in you that no one and no experience can shake.

8

Laugh It Off

I love to laugh. I would say I learned the trait from my mom, but really my entire family loves to laugh. I guess, with a last name like Doolittle, you learn to laugh early on in life. Sometimes laughter comes naturally; at other times it is a chosen response to tension or hurtful statements . . .

I was in technical rehearsals for a musical I was doing at the Boiler Room Theater in Franklin, Tennessee. That kind of rehearsal can be really stressful. We were trying to run through the entire show with the lighting cues, and it was not going well at all. At the end of the very last scene, the cast exited the stage and the director called for a blackout.

We stood offstage waiting for the lights to go down, but they never did. We were all tired, and we all wanted to go home. The director started to get angry. The only thing we had left to rehearse was the curtain call.

The director yelled, "BLACKOUT! I said BLACKOUT!"

I knew he was struggling to hold it together. Continuing to yell, he finally said in his angriest tone yet, "All I'm asking for is a blackout on stage. CAN I GET A BLACKOUT ON STAGE?"

So I ran out and stood right in the middle of the stage. It took him about two seconds to recognize that his only black cast member had made his wish a reality. Everyone burst out laughing, and rehearsal was officially over for the night. To this day, my nickname at that theater is "Blackout."

It is great to have friends who love to laugh as much as you do. My three background singers—Janet, Kelley, and Amy—also happen to be three of my best friends. My girls and I have so much fun on the road, and we are always able to find the humor in the all-too-frequent stressful situations.

For instance, I performed at a large corporate event with a house band, one I had never worked with previously. Fortunately, I was able to bring my girls along to sing background. We had one rehearsal with the band, the night before the event, and it went pretty well. I was unsure about one song, so I told the band to be prepared: I might decide to take it out of the first set. Other than that, we left rehearsal feeling confident that the show would go well the next day.

I should mention as a side note, because it's crucial to the story, that Janet, Kelley, and Amy are my "white divas," while most of the band members, including the bandleader, were black.

So, it's the day of the event, and we start performing. None of the songs are as we rehearsed. At one point, a song began and I wasn't even sure which song it was! As a result, I removed the song I had been unsure about and had mentioned to the band the night before. We made it through the first set, and thankfully the audience didn't seem to notice any problems.

During the break, the band was in one room, and we girls were in our own room. "I'm going to go over there and discuss some changes with the band," I told the girls. "Maybe we can figure out how to make the second set gel."

I went next door to inform the bandleader of my ideas. "Can we go over the next set to make sure we're straight?" I asked him.

"Please," he said. "Since you changed things up on me this last set."

I looked back at him in disbelief. *The band didn't play a single song the same as the night before, and he was saying something to me?* But I let it go and proceeded to rearrange the set in hopes that our set would go better the second time around.

When I went back and told the girls about our conversation, they were incredulous. "Are you kidding me?" Kelley asked in amazement.

Amy was flabbergasted. "I can't believe *he* would say that to *you!* That's like the pot calling the kettle . . ." Amy stopped abruptly, her words hanging in midair and her eyes wide with embarrassment. "Umm . . . Whatever!" Amy finally blurted out. We all screamed with laughter, realizing that she just couldn't manage to say the word *black* in this situation. We fell out of the room laughing, knowing that we were going to have fun performing the next set, no matter what. And we did!

Say What?

I went grocery shopping with Kelley one day, and we barely made it into the store when someone stopped us. The woman was apparently a worker in the store bakery and seemed excited to greet us. However, her first question to me was "Are you feeling better today?"

At first I was a bit confused. Then she went on to explain, "You came into the store a couple weeks ago, and one of our workers said, 'Is that Melinda Doolittle?' Another worker answered, 'I'm not sure.' They both turned to me, and I quickly said, 'Of course that's her. She just looks like crap today.'"

Kelley and I looked at each other and burst into laughter. How else do you respond to something like that?

People Say the Darndest Things!

Often, at "meet and greets" after my concerts, people say and do the strangest things. I've had people forget their names or their loved ones' names. A woman once asked me to sign something for her daughter. "Sure, what's her name?"

The woman looked back at me in abject horror. "I can't remember."

I thought, *Oh, this poor woman. She must have just had her baby recently, and she can't recall the baby's name.* Trying to ease the awkwardness, I asked, "How old is your daughter?"

"Twenty-one," she replied.

Sometimes after concerts, I feel as though I need an interpreter to translate the intentions behind a person's comments. A couple years ago, I met a woman who had waited in a very long line to talk to me. By the look on her face, I knew she had something important to tell me, but I had no idea what to expect. When she finally got to the signing table, she asked, "Are you the girl who sang on CeCe Winans' *Throne Room* CD? Are you the *Throne Room* girl?"

I hesitantly nodded. "Well," she continued, "my friend's son was eight years old, had cancer, and died listening to you sing!"

I wasn't sure whether to apologize or thank her for the story . . .

Then there was the signing that occurred right after I hurt my back pretty badly. The doctor had given me a muscle relaxant to ease the pain while I was on the road. This particular night the pain was really intense, so I took one-quarter of a pill right after the show and then went out to do the signing. I soon discovered that I don't handle muscle relaxants very well. The true proof of that came when a little boy handed me his picture to sign, and I asked him what his name was. He said, "Ben."

"Matt?" I replied.

"No. Ben," he said.

"M-A-T-T?" I spelled.

"No! B-E-N!" He spelled back. I knew right then that the muscle relaxant was not my friend. Thankfully, Ben and I were able to laugh about it at the end.

I've also had people run up to me and say, "You're not fat! I thought you were really fat when I saw you on TV." Or they say, "You're not ugly! They pegged you as the ugly one on *American Idol*."

Moments like these always make me laugh because I know that people sometimes say things without thinking. And I wonder if there will be a moment later in the day when they realize what they said, and that makes me laugh too. Everyone has those "I can't believe I did that" moments, and you can either let them eat you up, or you can choose to see the humor.

Thankful and Grateful

Mom never wanted me to be prideful or arrogant, so she refused to tell me that she was proud of me. Instead, she'd say, "I am thankful and I am grateful." Even now she winces slightly when people approach her and say, "Oh, you must be so proud of Melinda!" Mom gently corrects them, saying, "I am thankful and I am grateful." While it would have been nice to hear Mom say the words, "I'm proud of you," her reluctance to even hint at pride was her way of reminding me of the true source of my talent.

When I was invited to sing at the White House for President George W. Bush, it was a huge honor for me, so of course I took Mom along. As Mom and I were being introduced at the president's function, President Bush interrupted and said, "I know who this is. This is Melinda Doolittle and Mommy Doolittle."

Mom was thrilled. "He knows my name!" she whispered under her breath to me.

"Umm, he called you *Mommy*," I whispered in reply.

When Mom shook President Bush's hand, he said to her, "You must be so proud of your daughter."

Oh no! I thought. *The* p *word!*

The president had barely gotten the words out of his mouth when Mom raised her index finger in front of the president's face and gently replied, "I am *thankful* and I am *grateful*."

"Mom," I whispered after the president moved on, "you do realize that you just corrected the President of the United States."

Because of that moment, "thankful and grateful" has become a running joke with Mom and me. And never one to let a good joke go, I got my mom good when I played at Feinstein's, a highly regarded dinner-show venue in New York. Feinstein's uses a prerecorded message to introduce their performers each night. I did a six-show run there in the fall of 2009, and each night the message said, "Feinstein's is proud to present . . . Melinda Doolittle!"

Mom was able to come to one of the last shows in the

run, and I knew I had to do something special. I went to Jimmy, who was running the sound, and asked, "Can you change the prerecorded intro tonight?" He looked at me a little funny, but when I told him the story, he was completely game.

That night, as I was about to walk onto the stage and start my opening number, the lights dimmed and an announcement went out over the crowd: "Feinstein's is proud to present . . . No, wait . . . Feinstein's is *thankful* and *grateful* to present . . . Melinda Doolittle!" I heard a scream and then some stifled laughter, and I knew it was mission accomplished!

9

Do It Afraid

Have you ever had a challenge you were afraid to face? Fear can sometimes paralyze you, but if you choose to face your fear head on, you may be surprised by what you can accomplish . . .

When I went to the launch of The LEAGUE program in New York, I was accompanied by Secretary of Education Margaret Spellings, Nicole Lapin from CNN, and a player from the Harlem Globetrotters. We had already spent the day with the children and were on our way to the final event of the day. Members of the New York press and CNN were waiting for us outside. We filed onto a platform built especially for the occasion. I still wasn't sure what we were supposed to do there, but I soon found out.

Before I let you in on the rest of the story, I should tell you that I am really, *really*, REALLY afraid of birds for some reason. I'm not sure if I was traumatized as a child or what, but I normally scream and run anytime a bird gets slightly close to me. Well, when we got to the platform in front of the press, I was told that there was a special surprise for all the children and that I was supposed to present it. The surprise was . . . the release of twenty doves!

I quickly ran across the platform to the largest person I could find, the Globetrotter. I begged him to take over my duties for me. He was glad to do it, but the organizers of the event would not hear of it. They wanted *me* to release the doves as the cameras flashed and news channels filmed the entire thing.

I was petrified, but I had to find a way to face this challenge head on. So I asked the enormous basketball player to stand behind me with his hand on my back, so I wouldn't run away in fear. He agreed to do all he could to hold me in place.

The countdown began, and I was shaking all over. When the time came, the Globetrotter placed his hands on my back, and I leaned against them with all my might. As I lifted the cover off the doves and they began to fly, I screamed the loudest scream I have ever heard, but with a huge smile on my face. The pictures in the paper the next day showed me looking as though I was uncontrollably excited.

And I was! I had done it! I had faced my fear head on. I did it afraid, but I did it!

Stepping Out of My Comfort Zone

Life has offered me many opportunities to face my fears. During my senior year at Belmont, my voice teacher, Sandra Dudley, encouraged me to audition for the Commercial Music Showcase. This was a big deal at Belmont, since it was a full-scale stage event, complete with professional lighting, professional sound, and numerous representatives from the music industry in attendance. Only four artists would be selected to appear in the main event.

I didn't want to audition for the showcase, because—as I've shared—despite my experience singing background vocals, singing lead terrified me. Plus, I had sung background for a fellow student in the showcase the previous year and had a great time. I was content being in the background, but Sandra refused to allow me to remain behind the scenes. "I'm going to require you to do this audition as part of your grade," Sandra informed me. "It's time for you to step out of your comfort zone." I didn't feel that such coercive tactics were a nice way to play it, but they did the trick. I chose my two audition songs, booked some talented musician friends of mine, and scheduled a rehearsal. The first day I met with my band, I actually sat in the corner and cried while the band rehearsed the music. I was completely petrified even though all the members in the band were good friends of mine.

"Melinda, don't you want to sing along?" one of them asked, pointing to the microphone in the middle of the room that they had set up for me.

"Nope. What you're playing sounds great, but I really don't want to rehearse with the band." I was literally paralyzed with fear. I stayed in the room while the band rehearsed so I knew what to expect from them, but they had no idea what to expect from me. Jerry, the bass player and leader of the band, encouraged me: "Don't worry. You're going to be able to do it. We'll take it from here."

On the day of the audition, I stood outside the door to the audition room, shaking and second-guessing my decision to follow through with this. Then I reminded myself that if I didn't do the audition or didn't do it well, it wouldn't just reflect badly on me; it would make Sandra look bad too. That's when I decided to show the judges that I had a wonderful teacher who had prepared me well.

The audition took place in front of several professors sitting at tables as judges, very similar to the way the judges sit on *American Idol*. Everything about the audition went well, and a few hours later I received a call informing me that I had been chosen to be in Belmont's Commercial Music Showcase! I worked hard to get ready for the showcase. Belmont even brought in a "movement coach" to help me look and be more comfortable on stage. I put aside my fears of rehearsing with the band because I knew I needed to do the full-blown rehearsal if I hoped to do a good job. That was a turning point for me. Also, I realized—with the showcase musical director's help—that music was my calming agent. The director suggested that, rather than going onstage as soon as my name was announced, I stand offstage while the band started playing. I could calm down a bit and then walk on singing. It was a great plan!

The actual showcase took place in Massey Hall on the Belmont campus. In addition to leaders in Nashville's music industry, my entire family came to watch me perform in the Commercial Music Showcase. I closed the show and had an incredible time. I was still scared, but once the music started, I knew that I could do it. I ended up making some good contacts and getting more studio work because of the showcase. A few songwriters talked to me about singing demos for them, and I got some jobs singing background vocals. But most of all, I came away from the show knowing that I had taken huge steps toward conquering a fear I had battled for years. I had done it afraid!

Scary But Rewarding

When I wasn't on the road singing background, my favorite hobby was performing in musicals in local theater productions. I love playing a character. I can be onstage singing a solo and be completely calm about it. For some reason, when I was playing a character, there was no pressure. If the audience didn't like something I did, I could blame it on the character, and I would be far removed from their disapproval. I loved the freedom I felt when acting.

Once, I was working in a show at The Boiler Room, and during one of the first rehearsals, I met a guy named Doug Cordes. We quickly became good friends. Doug and I loved to hang out together during downtime, and we enjoyed talking and laughing about life. Doug was such a bright spot in my days. He and I were both at a point in our lives where we were ready for something to change. Doug wanted to pursue either a solo music career or performance on another level, and I was considering working for more mainstream music artists. I had done gospel most of my career, so making such a move was a big step for me. We were both a little scared but excited about the possibilities.

Then one night Doug came in talking about auditions for *American Idol.* I didn't know much about the audition process, but like millions of other music lovers, I had watched *American Idol*, a sort of interactive televised talent contest, with viewers casting votes by telephone or text messages during or immediately after each show. Performers were critiqued by three judges: at the time, renowned recording producer Randy Jackson; recording artist Paula Abdul; and music executive and entrepreneur Simon Cowell. Each week one more performer was voted off the program, the remainder went on to compete the following week, and the last one standing was declared the new "American Idol." Auditions were held each year in various arenas and stadiums around the country, with more than two hundred thousand singers aspiring to the title.

Doug was from Alabama, and the next audition was scheduled in Birmingham. When Doug asked if I wanted to go with him, my first response was NO!

I was convinced that my next career move would still involve singing background vocals, and that was where I was comfortable. But Doug was relentless; he kept urging me to consider the *American Idol* auditions. He reminded me about all the fun aspects of the audition—seeing the costumes, hearing the crazy auditions firsthand, all the while hanging out with my buddy. I slowly warmed to the idea, and I finally said I was in.

I immediately called my best friend and vocal coach, Janet, told her about our plans, and asked her if she knew something I should sing. She asked me what my favorite song was, and I told her anything by Stevie Wonder made me smile. We decided on "For Once in My Life." Then she said I should probably have another song prepared just in case. I explained to her that I was too scared to think about that.

Unfortunately, the Birmingham auditions fell on a show day for Doug and me, so we scrapped our plans. I was relieved, because the actual audition part scared me. The next day, however, Doug came backstage with excitement in his eyes as he informed me that the last *American Idol* audition city that year was Memphis, and it was scheduled on one of our days off from work.

"Great!" I said to him as my stomach began to do somersaults. I didn't want Doug to know how scared I was, so I invited along some distractions: my friends Christy and Missi joined our twosome. It worked out perfectly. Christy's dad and stepmom lived on the outskirts of Memphis and invited us to stay with them. We hopped into Christy's car and headed to Memphis. I successfully hid my nervousness by focusing on the thoughts that I'd see some people wearing funny costumes and that I was with great friends.

We pulled into Memphis and headed straight to the FedEx Forum to pick up the *American Idol* wristbands that identified us as contestants. By this point, I was panicking inwardly and seriously considering just observing the event instead of actually singing. But when we walked into the registration area, I discovered that *American Idol* didn't allow observers except for guardians of minors. *Do it afraid!* I reminded myself. I checked in and got my wristband.

American Idol had allotted two registration days, and since we showed up on the evening of the first day, we had the next day free. We had a blast! We toured Memphis, went out to eat, and pretty much spent the day laughing about our wristband escapades. You see, the AI staff puts a paper wristband on each contestant at the registration site and then explains that the wristband needs to remain intact until your audition. That means it can't get torn or wet. Needless to say, we experienced pretty comedic showers that day. They involved Ziploc bags and duct tape. That's all I will say.

We had so much fun that day that I almost forgot about being scared. In fact, for the first time, I was actually looking forward to what was ahead.

Christy's stepmom asked us to sing our audition songs

for her since she couldn't be at the arena the next day. I let my friends go first, so I could work up the nerve. They were amazing! Normally, that would have made me more nervous, but this time it actually calmed me. We had our team together, I wasn't alone, and we were going to make it fun. I happily sang my song, and we got ready to turn in early. We needed to be at the venue by 4:45 a.m. the next day. Before we went to bed, though, I decided to do one more thing I thought might encourage us for the next day. I called my friend Mandisa. She was performing on the *American Idol Live* Tour for Season Five and was just finishing a show. Excited that we were braving the audition process, Mandisa encouraged all of us. Now motivated for our big day, we all went to bed early.

We were up at three o'clock the next morning. I was in charge of bringing the tickets that determined our audition order, and we were on our way by 4:00. However, we had to turn around and head right back to the house, because *someone* had forgotten the tickets. Now I was getting scared again. Apparently my brain wasn't working real well, so I fretted that it might be a long, long day.

We arrived at the arena on time—it was a miracle—and were shocked to see so many people there. And the crowd did not disappoint. There were hilarious costumes, larger-than-life personalities, and people singing their tails off. It was unlike anything I had ever seen. Despite my nervousness, I was instantly glad we had come. As we filed in with sixteen thousand other competitors, we had no idea how long our day would be.

Twelve hours later, after hearing everyone in the arena practicing and auditioning, it was our turn. We had seen and heard literally thousands of people we thought sounded pretty good, but they dejectedly headed to what we called the "walk of shame," the long staircase that led a rejected contestant out of the building. In an odd sort of way, seeing so many fine vocalists eliminated relieved some pressure. After all, I didn't have any lofty expectations. I was just glad to be finally auditioning.

The event producers placed the singers who were auditioning into groups of four. Doug and Christy were in my group, and Missi was in the group right next to us. There were a few groups in front of us, so as they auditioned, I had time to actually think about what I was getting ready to do. That's when I got scared. Really scared. I had to remind myself of the "Do it afraid" motto I had been reciting. I told myself it was only a thirty-second audition and that I could do it even if I had to do it afraid. I was so nervous that my legs were shaking and my knees were literally knocking together.

Finally, it was our turn to audition. Missi, who was in the group next to us, went first. Her voice rang out like a trumpet in the arena. She was amazing, as usual, so I figured she was in, that she would be asked to continue in the audition process. As the rest of her group sang, the producers began calling on my group. The young woman at the end of our line went first, then Christy, then Doug. Christy and Doug nailed their songs. I was so excited. But just as I got ready to sing, I saw an *American Idol* producer send Missi the wrong direction. She was walking up those dreaded stairs to exit the building.

What? Missi eliminated? That can't be! I didn't know what to think. I was so upset. When it was my turn to sing, I must have channeled that nervous anger into my song, because I sang the Stevie Wonder hit "For Once in My Life" with all my might. The producer looked at me for a second with a blank stare and then said, "Sing something else."

The first song that popped into my head was the old classic "My Funny Valentine." I sang a bit, and he stared again.

"Sing something else."

Now I was panicking. *Why did everybody else only do one song and I was getting ready to do my third?* I tried to think of a song I knew well, but everything escaped my mind except for the Chaka Khan song, "Tell Me Something Good." I went for it. If I had been thinking clearly, I would never have picked that song, because it has long spaces of downtime between the lines of the verse and chorus. Standing in front of the producer, I would sing a line and then, bopping my head to the imaginary music, wait for what seemed like forever for the next line to come. By the time I got to the chorus, I looked at the producer and decided to change the lyric a bit. "Tell me that you *like* me," I sang.

His blank stare cracked, a slight smile broke out, and he said, "You're through." It took me a second to realize that he meant only me, not Doug and Christy.

"What?" Before I could ask any further questions, the *Idol* ushers pointed my friends and me in opposite directions. I headed to another section of the arena to find out what I was to do next, and my friends climbed the arena stairs. The *Idol* staff explained that I would be coming back for another audition in two days. They handed me a form to sign and sent me on my way. Everything happened so quickly, I didn't even have time to figure out if I was excited or scared. All I knew was that I wanted to find my friends. Even though they were disappointed about not making it through to the next level of auditions, they were so excited for me. I tried my best to follow suit, but I couldn't shake my fear. I made up my mind at that moment that I would not be going back to any auditions for *American Idol*. It was just too scary. I was proud of myself for making it as far as I had, and that was plenty fulfilling for me.

Almost giddy with fatigue, my friends and I went to dinner and talked and laughed about how crazy our day had been. Christy's dad and his wife even came and hung out with us. Once they saw that Christy was okay with the results, they were ultra-excited for me. I appreciated their kind comments, but I was still afraid to proceed any further with *American Idol* auditions. I didn't sleep much that night. I knew that if I didn't go to the next audition, I would be running away from a great opportunity, but at the same time I couldn't shake the dread. So the next morning I hopped in the car with my friends and headed back to Nashville. We had a fun drive home, and by the time I walked in my front door, I had convinced myself that I had conquered my fear of stepping out and singing lead simply by going to that first audition. I was golden! What I hadn't anticipated was communicating that message to my mother. She was quiet for a few seconds, and then she gently asked, "Did you sign anything while you were there?"

I explained that I had, but that it wasn't a big deal. "It was just a release form for television, really."

Mom waited another couple of seconds and then asked, "Did it mention anything about the next audition?"

I cautiously answered, "It mentioned the date, but that was it." Then I quickly added, "I'm sure they don't expect everyone who signed the form to actually come back. They must anticipate that some people may not be able to return for another audition."

This time my mother's voice was not as gentle. "Honey, we are women of our word, so if you signed something about the next audition, you need to go!"

I was trapped. Mom had raised me to keep my word, and this situation was no exception. Since I had signed an agreement, I had to go through with it, no matter how scared I was. I didn't even bother telling my mom about my fears, because I knew she was right. What I did not know, however, was that my audition was an answer to Mom's prayers. Months later, she confessed to having prayed for several years that I would audition for *American Idol*, but anytime she brought it up, I would shoot it down. She didn't want to nag about it, so she didn't. She just kept praying.

American Idol limits contestants to under twenty-nine years of age, so when I accepted Doug's invitation to go to the audition, a mere two months before my twenty-ninth birthday, Mom knew this was her answer. Had I been aware she was praying that way, I would have known that my path was already set. I was going to audition for *American Idol* and go as far as the judges and the viewers would let me.

The Judges' Round

The final audition took place in front of Simon Cowell, Paula Abdul, and Randy Jackson, that season's highly opinionated *American Idol* judges. I was able to bring four people along with me to the audition site as my "support group." I chose carefully: I took my praying Mommy; my best friend and vocal coach, Janet; Doug, the one who started it all; and Dwayne Parker, one of my closest friends and my hugest encourager. I knew that if I were to have any chance at squashing the fear inside me, I needed the right people with me.

The audition was an early-morning slot, so Janet made sure I was warmed up and ready. Doug understood what I was going through and held my hand. Dwayne kept saying, "You got this! I'm so excited!" Meanwhile, I panicked and my mom prayed. When we walked into the holding room and I saw others waiting for their turn to audition, I calmed down a little bit. We were all in this together, and it was going to be okay. Simon, Paula, and Randy came into the room to give us a brief pep talk. Randy said, "You can do this. You just have to be you."

Paula offered some kind words of encouragement. "I know this is scary," she said, "but everything is going to be okay."

Then Simon added, "Don't mess up."

I was no longer calm.

As the judges left the room, people began frantically practicing and making sure they knew their songs. I fought to keep the panic from overwhelming me. The next thing I knew, I was asked to interview with one of the producers. He asked how I was feeling.

"I'm waiting to go in to audition today," I answered, "and I have a level of excitement, and I'm just trying to sit on my hands to stop the rest of the shaking that's going along with that." The cameraman laughed, but I wasn't joking. I really was nervous. It truly was the most scared I had ever been. I realized, though, that I needed to do this. I couldn't be afraid of stepping out of the background all my life. I had to conquer my fears, and that knowledge kept me going.

Still, my nervousness continued. And to top it all off, my contestant number would not stick to the vest I was wearing. I had chosen to wear blue jeans with a beige T-shirt, hat, and vest. But the material of the vest was such that the 5 x 8 inch sticky paper would not adhere to it.

Already nervous, I kept pressing on the paper, trying to

get the number to stay put. I was still shaking when my name was called and I bounded through the double doors into the audition room. Sandwiched between a large red *American Idol* backdrop and a large blue *American Idol* backdrop was a simple table where Randy, Paula, and Simon sat. They were leaning back in their studio-control-room-style chairs and looking a lot more comfortable than I felt. The infamous Simon Cowell gnawed idly on the end of his pen. They looked friendly and innocuous, yet somehow terribly intimidating to me.

Almost immediately when I took my place in front of the red backdrop, my number fell off. I picked it up and tried desperately to pat it back in place several times before Simon said, "It's okay. Forget about the number."

The judges asked some questions about my singing experience, specifically why I enjoyed singing background rather than lead. "Being in the background is my comfort zone," I told them.

"So what changed?" asked Simon, implying the rest of the question as to why I would be auditioning as a lead singer.

"I know I need to get over my fear of standing in front of people."

"Okay," Simon nodded.

"What are you singing?" asked Randy.

"'For Once in My Life.'"

"I love that song," Randy said.

Great, I thought. *Now he'll know if I mess up.* I took a deep breath as the judges sat staring at me. My hands were still shaking as I started singing, but once I got into the song, my hands began expressing the lyrics along with my voice. Simon sat up and leaned forward, his gaze riveted on me; Randy sat back, smiling; and Paula sat up straight, hands in front of her face, her legs crossed under the table.

I finished the song, and there was a brief moment of silence that seemed like an eternity as I stared straight ahead at the judges.

Paula was the first to speak . . . sort of. "Mmm," she said, nodding her head.

"Wow," Randy said softly. "What do you think, Paula?"

Paula looked at me as she spoke. "You're good. You're really good. You've got to believe, though."

I smiled back at her. "My hands are still shaking."

"You were scared to death," Randy interjected.

Simon leaned back in his chair and held his pen close to his face. "Melinda," he began, "we have a lot of people who come in here with a lot of attitude and a lot of confidence, and they're not very good. You walk in with no confidence, no attitude, and yet you are a brilliant singer. A brilliant singer. Seriously."

"Thank you," I mouthed the words, but no sound came

out. I was truly amazed at Simon's kind compliment, and I guess it showed in my countenance.

"Look at that look on your face," Paula said.

The look of surprise on my face would come to be well known by *Idol* fans over the next few months. It was real that day, and it remained real right to the end.

Simon continued, "You are what it's all about—a great voice. I am concerned about the lack of confidence, about the fact that you've been in the background. But let me tell you, you are in the top 2 percent of good singers this year. One million percent, yes."

Simon pitched the critique to the only female judge on the show at the time. "Paula?"

"I think you are brilliant. Yes," Paula echoed Simon.

Randy picked up from there. "I think you are sensational. One of the best auditions ever, vocally."

"I agree," said Simon.

"Welcome to Hollywood!" Randy shouted, his arms wide open, and then he began clapping his hands.

I jumped up and down in glee, then stooped down and picked up my fallen contestant number. A staffer handed me the coveted golden ticket, indicating that I had been invited to Hollywood, and I danced out the door. As I was exiting the room, Randy called out behind me, "Believe in yourself, man. Come on! You know you got it!" His voice was overshadowed by the screams and squeals of my mom, Janet, Doug, Dwayne, and others in the hallway as I ran into their arms waving my golden ticket.

Mom was in full worship mode, dancing and giving praise and honor to God with her hands high in the air. She always gets excited about answered prayer.

When we finally calmed down, we went out to eat, and for the first time it really struck me: *I might be on the show!* I hadn't known what to expect when I first auditioned for *American Idol*, and it all seemed like a fun but frightening experiment. But after successfully getting through the audition and making it to Hollywood, it slowly dawned on me, *Okay, maybe I am supposed to be here. And if I'm here, I want to do the absolute best I can every step of the way!* I learned a valuable lesson that day. You'll never know what you can do if you don't try, if you don't step out, believing you can do anything. Sure, we're all tempted to hang back. They don't call it a "comfort zone" for no reason. It is the place of least resistance, the known rather than the unknown, the tried and true rather than the risky. It is the place we can continue to operate easily without rocking the boat.

But if we are ever to experience new levels of freshness and excitement in our lives, we sometimes have to step out of the boat despite our fears and embrace the unexpected. For me, stepping out of the boat meant stepping out of the background and singing in front of Paula, Randy, and Simon—and then millions of other people.

What might stepping out of the boat mean for you? When you muster up the courage to do so, remember that success is not measured by the lack of fear. Success is measured by your choice to do it anyway. If you have to, do it afraid!

10

Give It All You've Got

American Idol's Hollywood Week was the most traumatic five days I've ever lived through. From all across the country, the nearly two hundred contestants who had survived the local auditions traveled to Hollywood to engage in an intense weeklong competition to determine who would advance toward an appearance on the televised show.

Every person there was pursuing a dream, so we had the common bond of being out of our element in the surreal world of a big-time television production. Even though we were in competition, we formed fast friendships. Knowing that the purpose of the week was to whittle the number of contestants down to the Top 40 was definitely a strain on everyone, so we needed one another. The rehearsal and activity schedules were relentless and the pressure so intense that I lost eight pounds in one week, something I had never done before in my life and may never do again!

Hollywood Week took place at the beautifully lavish Orpheum Theater, a Los Angeles landmark since the days of Judy Garland. It really was "Lights, camera, action!"—and the action was primarily provided by us.

Although I had sung in studios and concert halls, I had never before been in an environment quite like this—with camera operators, sound guys, makeup artists, and production assistants with their clipboards, all looking as though they were on life-or-death missions as they swirled through the area where we were to perform. I walked around like the proverbial kid in a candy store: I was wide-eyed with amazement.

The week began with each contestant appearing before judges Randy, Paula, and Simon to sing a cappella and explain why he or she should be the next American Idol. That was difficult for me, because only a few weeks earlier I had been struggling just to get over my fear of stepping out and going to the auditions. I was happy and content being a background singer; I wasn't very confident in my skills beyond that.

So rather than give the impression that I knew I could win the contest, I decided to simply have fun. During our long wait in the audition line in Memphis, my three friends and I had written a short, silly *American Idol* theme song using the letters of the show's name, so when the judges asked me the inevitable question, I was ready. "I should be the next American Idol," I said, "because I've written your next theme song." I launched into the song: "A to the M to the E to the R; to the I can! I do; L."

Randy and Simon cracked up laughing, and Paula applauded. Thankfully, that broke the ice and calmed me down enough to sing my a cappella song for that round, "All Is Fair in Love." Unfortunately, the judges were unimpressed. At that point they were sick of hearing slow songs, so my choice of material left them cold. And everything I did with that song was wrong.

"You're going to have to do better than that," Simon warned. "We're going to let you through, but if you don't bring it, you're going home."

His blunt statement made me nervous as I anticipated the next round—until I found out it was Group Day. During that round, the contestants were placed in groups of four to perform one song we selected from a list of four song choices provided by the producers. In addition to being part of the ensemble, each person in the group was required to sing a solo at some point in the song. For many contestants, this experience was extremely stressful, but I loved it because it gave me the chance to draw on my background singing. I was in my comfort zone. We weren't given the assignment until 9:00 p.m. "At seven in the morning, we start," the *Idol* staffer told us.

Unlike some other *Idol* group performances, we were able to choose our group members for this segment of the competition. The group I chose was tremendous: there was my roommate, Tammy the amazing rocker, plus roommates Nicole and Sarah. Not liking drama and determined to get some sleep that night, we got right down to business. One of the girls was a choreographer, so she helped us with our moves. Tammy was a songwriter, so she helped teach us the arrangement. I used my background singing to help with harmonies. By one o'clock in the morning, we had our song ready, and the next day we nailed it. The judges said we were one of the best groups that day.

Because everyone in our group did so well, all four of us passed through to the next level of the competition. We were so excited! There were only a few groups that day in which all of the members advanced to the next round. The judges listened to a group and then decided which individuals, if any, they wanted to keep. The others were sent home.

By the last day of the competition, the number of remaining contestants was dwindling rapidly, and I couldn't believe I was still hanging in there. Simon's admonition had motivated me to bring my best effort every time I sang.

For our last audition, we were given eight songs from which to choose one to perform, and this time we would be accompanied by a piano and background singers.

Before Hollywood Week, I had picked out a perfectly fitting white suit to wear just in case I made it to the final auditions, but because I had lost so much weight, the suit felt loose and frumpy. I was exhausted, my voice was tired, and I wasn't looking too cute, but I made it through my song. I wondered if I had done enough to impress the judges. At this point in the competition, though, the judges said nothing to the contestants about our performances. It was simply a matter of singing and then going to one of three large hotel rooms with other contestants to await the results. Twenty contestants were assigned to each room, and it was an all-or-nothing decision. Every contestant in two of the rooms would continue to the next level of judging, and none of the contestants in the third room would be invited back to the competition.

After the sixty of us had sung our final song, I was ushered into a room with nineteen other contestants, many of whom were sitting on the floor, propped up against a wall, or stretched out in the middle of the room, nervously talking among themselves. As I quickly glanced around the room, I tried to recall some of the performances I'd heard by those individuals I recognized. Had we done well—or had we not done as well as the judges expected? Everyone in the hotel room was looking at one another, wondering if this was one of the groups that would be invited back. The cameraman caught every bit of our anxiety.

After what seemed like hours, the door opened, and in walked Paula, Simon, and Randy. I was sitting on the floor, and as Paula began to speak, I did what I normally do when I'm scared—I closed my eyes and put my head down until it was over.

"It's been an interesting road," Paula began slowly and deliberately. "We've had some highlighted moments. We've had some near fatal moments." She paused and let her words sink into our hearts. "You're all aware of how many rooms we have, correct?" We hardly dared nod. Paula paused again, and the silence in the room created a heavy shroud. Then Paula smiled and said, "Congratulations."

The twenty contestants in our room had made it to the Top 40! We lost our minds screaming and hugging one another. After Paula, Simon, and Randy stayed for a couple minutes to congratulate us, they exited the room and moved on down the hall to inform another group of twenty contestants that they had made it—and twenty others that they had not.

No Longer a Backup Singer

At the end of Hollywood Week, everyone headed home. I felt pretty good about how I had handled the pressure. I had taken more steps toward overcoming my fear, and I was happy about that. I actually started to get excited about what might lie ahead.

The Top 40 returned to California in January 2007 for the Green Mile day. By this time, my great friend Dwayne had moved to Los Angeles, so he accompanied me and helped boost my confidence. During that day, nobody sang; nobody performed at all. It was simply a day of judgment at which the Top 24 are announced. Walking slowly down the hardwood floor, I made my way to the waiting judges. My legs were shaking so badly, I needed all my concentration to simply make it to my position without falling. I hadn't realized I could ever be that nervous.

Their faces expressionless, Paula, Randy, and Simon sat in their usual places at the judges' table. All three of them were concealing any hint of what might be coming next. First Paula and Randy offered kind words of encouragement, and then Simon took over.

"Melinda Doolittle, basically there's a reason why you are a backup singer," he began, "because, normally, someone is better than you." I had no idea where Simon was going with his statement, and my heart was in my throat. "You may be surprised," Simon continued, "when I tell you that you are good enough to stand at the front of the stage, and you are through to the next round."

I wanted to say thank you, but no words seemed to come out of my mouth as I leaned forward and buried my face in my hands. When I lifted my head, I was wearing a huge smile.

"This was unanimous, kid. You are no longer a backup singer," Simon added. "Got that?"

"I got it," I managed to reply.

"Come here." Simon nodded as he got up, came around the table, and hugged me. "I'm really pleased with you," he said.

I could barely contain myself! I got back into the elevator and cried the entire ride down to the ground level. I walked into the room where Ryan Seacrest, Dwayne, and some other contestants were waiting. I gave them a two-thumbs-up signal, and they burst into cheers and screams. I had made it through all the initial rounds of auditions. I was definitely going to sing on *American Idol*. But that incredible opportunity set up an interesting scenario. I now had twelve days to go home, pack, tie up loose ends, and be back in Los Angeles for the start of the show. As one of the Top 24, I would be appearing on television for some part of the sixth season, but how much of it? I might be there for one week, or I could be there for several months. There are no guarantees with *American Idol*—only opportunities.

But would I actually be able to make the cut and stay for the full thirteen-week season? Should I put my life on hold for three months and turn down any singing opportunities on the road and in the studio? Should I move out of my home? What if I pull up stakes in Nashville, fail in Los Angeles, and then have nothing to go back to? Even if things go well, how am I going to pay my bills? A million questions pummeled my mind.

Making matters more complicated, I knew that I'd be going to L.A. for *American Idol*, but by contract, I was not permitted to tell anyone, including potential employers. The identity of the Top 24 was to remain a secret until that episode aired on television. The penalty for leaking the information was removal from the competition. So, when Martha Munizzi asked me to go on tour with her early in 2007, I didn't know what to tell her. I couldn't tell her about *Idol*, so I simply said, "I have something coming up, and I may or may not be able to do it, so if you need to fill that position now, you probably should get someone else." I loved working with Martha, but I didn't want to inconvenience her if I happened to do well enough to stay on *American Idol* for an extended period of time.

I was still wondering where this would lead as the music and lights came up on the stage for the first of three nationally broadcast semifinal eliminations. The show drew an enormous television audience of nearly 38 million viewers. I tried not to think about that, though, or my fear might paralyze me. For my first song, I sang "(Sweet Sweet Baby) Since You've Been Gone," and I had the time of my life! After seeing myself as a background singer for so long, I now had an entire band and a fabulous group of background singers behind me! It was an invigorating feeling, and I sang with tremendous freedom.

Following my performance, the judges were enthusiastic. Randy was unrestrained in his praise: "You blew it out of the box! All you need is to have confidence and believe in yourself, because you've got the natural gift. That was the bomb!"

"No more background singing. You are a frontrunner," Paula said, "and you are a firecracker too!"

Even Simon lathered on the praise. "Over two nights, I have seen people come out here with little talent and a huge amount of arrogance. And you are the opposite. You are an incredible singer, you have a fantastic story, you are a fantastic person. I really hope you do well."

On the second show I chose to sing "My Funny Valentine." It was one of my favorite songs, but I wasn't sure what the judges would think of the version I did. Surprisingly, they loved it. Paula gave me a standing ovation, and Randy once again enthusiastically praised my performance. It was Simon who really shocked me. "That," he paused and the entire studio fell silent, "was incredible. Without question, the best vocal we've had through the competition." Simon went on, "We've had some precocious little monsters on this show, with very little talent and enormous egos. You have this fantastic talent, great voice. What I like about you is that you don't know how good you are. And I don't think you are someone who would change if you did well. And I think this is part of your appeal. You are a breath of fresh air."

For my third song of the semifinals, I wasn't sure what I wanted to do. I thought about "Natural Woman," but another contestant was already singing that. Then I remembered a Prince song called "How Come You Don't Call Me." I figured no one would be singing that, so I turned it in. Wrong again! Someone else was already planning on doing that song. I needed a song that had a bang, but I couldn't think of anything.

I prayed and asked God to remind me of songs that I loved. Then it came to me: "I'm a Woman." I loved the attitude and the bluesy-ness of it, and I was excited because it had some power background vocals at the end, and the singers on the show were phenomenal. The song went over better than I hoped it would, drawing raves from Randy. "The hottest one of the night! You are the consummate pro! You are ready to go into the studio and make a record!"

Paula's comments were equally kind, and then Simon cracked up the audience by cocking his head, giving me a quasi-sultry look, and saying, "You little tiger." The audience roared in approval. "I thought we had a pussycat," Simon continued. "I loved that! Melinda, it is quite obvious. I don't need to tell you how good a singer you are, but it is very, very nice that you are actually enjoying every second you are having on this show. We hear previous contestants say, 'It was my stepping-stone.' But you are loving it, and so you should. This is your time in the spotlight." Then Simon offered his opinion on whether I would make it through the semifinal eliminations. "A million percent we're going to see you next week." And that's how I made it into the Top 12.

Starting Again from Scratch

Once the number of contestants was winnowed down to twelve, the format of the show changed a bit. It was almost as if we were starting over. Now, each week we had a theme and a special guest mentor with expertise in that week's theme. The mentors were wonderfully encouraging, easygoing, and quick to offer advice. Despite their laid-back manners, the fact that they were artists I admired intimidated me. The mentors during my season were Diana Ross, LuLu, Jon Bon Jovi, Martina McBride, Jennifer Lopez, Gwen Stefani, Barry Gibb, and Tony Bennett.

The first week of the Top 12 was Diana Ross week. I chose to sing "Home," one of my favorite songs from the popular movie musical *The Wiz*. Before meeting with Ms. Ross, I met with Deborah Byrd, one of the *American Idol* vocal coaches. We affectionately called her "Byrd," and she had been my rock during the competition. We had much in common as far as our musical styles and tastes, and working with her always made me excited about my performance. When I mentioned the song "Home," I saw the concerned look on her face. I immediately knew what she was thinking without her saying a word.

"Don't worry," I told her. "I will not be singing the part that says, 'I wish I was home. I wish I was back there.'"

Byrd sighed with relief. We both believed that words are powerful, and in a competition where American television viewers have the choice to send you *home*, it would not be the smartest thing to tell them you wished you were there.

Instead, we chose the lyrics that really explained what I felt at the time. Those words expressed how everything around me was changing, but I had learned so much in the process and knew this was where I was supposed to be. I had found my new "home" on that stage.

When I walked in the room to sing the song for Diana Ross, I was petrified, but I knew I had a story to tell, so I was also excited. As I sang the song, she seemed to follow along with every word. When I finished, she said, "I have chill bumps. You have just told your story with that song."

I wanted to cry, but I held in my tears. I was just happy she understood where I was coming from, and I could only hope the judges and the viewers heard the same thing.

When I stepped onto the stage to sing that week, I was ready to tell my story. What I didn't expect was for the entire studio audience to connect with it so quickly. They were on their feet even before I finished the song. I didn't know what to think. The tears weren't as easy to control at that point, so I let them go—and Paula cried with me. I had found my home, and it was in a place I had never even dared to dream of—on a stage in front of millions of people. And I was telling them my story . . .

I remember walking into the room for my mentor session during the Top 4 week and seeing Barry Gibb standing there.

Of course I was excited and nervous about singing his songs in front of him. We had two songs to choose that week, and it had been the hardest week for me by far. It had taken me quite awhile to choose my first song. I loved the song "Love You Inside and Out," but I wanted to make sure the lyrics were okay. Someone had mentioned that the lyrics were very sexual, and even though I hadn't interpreted the song that way, I wanted to make sure my thoughts were correct. I asked everyone I encountered, called my friends and family, and finally decided that the words were simply a wonderful description of love—and nothing more.

But I still hadn't chosen my second song. I listened to every Bee Gees song ever recorded, and I kept coming back to "How Can You Mend a Broken Heart." There was only one problem. It had a line in it that said, "How can a loser ever win?" I did not want to sing those words in this competition and essentially call myself a loser.

I went straight to Byrd with my dilemma, and she suggested that I just sing the first verse lyrics again at that point in the song and thereby avoid the negative line altogether. I thought Byrd's suggestion was a great idea—until I went to sing in front of Barry Gibb. I saw the confused look on his face the moment the changed line came out of my mouth, and the stymied expression stayed on Barry's face until the song was over. Then he took a deep breath and said, "You changed the lyrics and left out a pretty strong line on the song. Did you mean to do that?" I hesitated for one second before deciding to just come clean with him and explain my reasoning. He only answered with "Okay."

I wouldn't know what Barry Gibb thought about the change until I was getting ready to step onto the stage and perform the song on the live show. When they played the interview with him about my song, right before the end he said, "At first I didn't understand why Melinda changed the words to the song, but after she explained herself, I decided I wouldn't want to call myself a loser in this situation either."

I breathed a sigh of relief, sang my song, and continued on in the competition another week.

Believe in Yourself

Each mentor was extremely helpful, but I shared an exceptionally special experience with Tony Bennett when he listened to my arrangement of "I've Got Rhythm."

"You are a good singer," he told me. "You gotta believe in you." Mr. Bennett is a "singer's singer," the quintessential vocal stylist, so when he expressed his confidence in me, I was overjoyed. Thanks to his encouragement, I went on stage and sang my heart out. The audience responded with a long, standing ovation. Once again Randy Jackson raved, saying, "You know what I love? . . . You come out here every week, and you give everyone here a lesson in singing. You interpret the lyric. She sings with the feeling that the lyric portrays. This is how you do it, America!"

"I'll even up that," Paula exuded. "You're like a master class for everyone else to watch." I was shocked and speechless. How can a person even respond to such wonderful compliments? So I simply stood there with my shocked look on my face.

"I didn't like the first half of the song," Simon began his critique. "I thought it was a bit cabaret." Paula groaned, as did the audience, but Simon waved them off. "No, I liked the last part of the song," he attempted to say over the audience's noisy protests. "Oh, shut up!" Simon whimsically cajoled the crowd. "I thought the second half of the song was great. It was personality, fun." Simon looked at me and shrugged his shoulders as he said, "But I don't think we're ever going to be able to criticize you. This is a problem."

"Why?" Ryan Seacrest asked from the stage, echoed by Randy at the judges' table.

"Why is it a problem?" Ryan repeated his question so everyone could hear.

"Because we like being mean to people occasionally," Simon answered with a laugh.

"But not if they deserve the actual positive feedback," Ryan contended.

"Yes!" Randy agreed.

"Simon, you can't just be mean for the sake of being mean," Ryan playfully rebuked him.

"Yes, I can!" Simon replied, only half joking. And for the first time that night, my shocked look turned into a smile. Simon's honesty coupled with his wit had solidified his place as my favorite judge.

Tell the Story

A most amazing opportunity came during Week 7, when the entire program was designated as "Idol Gives Back." Because of the tenor of the show, contestants were asked to perform "inspirational" songs, which I was only too happy to do. I selected "There Will Come a Day," a song originally recorded by Faith Hill and one that gave me a natural opportunity to state my faith to millions of people.

One of the most challenging experiences for me came in Week 8: that was Rock Week, and I worked with Jon Bon Jovi to perform one of his songs, "Have a Nice Day." Now, I love all styles of music, but I've never considered myself a rocker, so I was uncomfortable and not quite sure what to do musically or even physically on stage. Jon was so sweet, and he promised to teach me how to rock. "You've already got soul," Jon told me. "You've got the pipes. You just have to own it." Jon gave me an unusual tip for performing the song: "Honey, take it to church. Raise your hands! Testify! It's church!"

"Okay," I said. "I like church."

Jon Bon Jovi helped allay my fears, and the performance went well despite my discomfort. Recognizing my uneasiness with the attitude of the lyrics, Paula nonetheless declared me a rock star. Randy and Simon compared me to a young Tina Turner.

Each week the competition grew more intense, and each week (except for the "Idol Gives Back" show) somebody else went home. It was tough to say good-bye to some of the young artists with whom I had become close friends over the weeks we were together. Yet at the same time, each week that I survived gave me another chance to influence an enormous audience.

On the *Idol* finale, when I discovered I was going to be singing "The Midnight Train to Georgia" with Gladys Knight, I seriously flipped out. I have listened to Gladys Knight as far back as I can remember. My dad let me listen to anything I wanted, but Mom was more cautious. She would let me listen to Christian music only, so I had to listen to Gladys

Knight while hiding under my bedcovers. But listen I did, and I was mesmerized by the woman. Something about her voice and the way she sings simply moves me. So to discover that Ms. Knight and I would be on the same show, singing together, was almost more than I could handle.

Following our first rehearsal, I literally dropped to my knees and started crying. Gladys came over and sat down by me. Putting her hand on my shoulder, she said, "What's wrong, Melinda?"

I looked up at her and said through my tears, "Do you know who you are?" Gladys smiled. "Well, thank you for caring," she replied sweetly.

We struck up a conversation, and I asked Ms. Knight for her advice. "What would you tell me?"

"I've been watching you," she said, "and I see how you tell a story with your music. When you sing a song, it is almost as though we can open up a book and read the story as you perform it. I've been singing for so long now that, over the years, I've passed the book stage, and now I try to express a movie in my songs."

Gladys Knight's encouragement set a new standard for me. From that moment on, I've tried to express a movie through my songs, so the listeners can see the images in their minds as I'm singing. In 2009, when my album *Coming Back to*

You was released and the *New York Times* music reviewers compared my singing to Gladys Knight, I nearly fainted. To even see my name in the same sentence with Ms. Knight's was such a high honor for me!

Keep Dreaming

One of the best lessons I learned from my experience on *American Idol* is to keep dreaming big. I never intended to audition for the show, but I'm so glad I did. I really feel that the experience forced me out of my comfort zone and allowed me to see another way God could take my dreams and make them bigger than I could ever imagine. Because of my *American Idol* journey, I have become stronger, and I am much more confident that performing as a solo artist is exactly what I'm supposed to be doing right now. And I want to pass that sort of confidence on to others. My goal is to encourage as many people as possible to dare to step out of their comfort zones and experience the very best life has to offer.

11

Lose to Win

We live in a world that exalts and praises winners. Rarely do you see an athlete on television raising two fingers and shouting at the camera, "We're number two!" No, we all want to be number one; we want to be the best, to be in the winner's circle, to be the star, the American Idol, the person whose name is up in lights. But sometimes you don't have to be number one to win . . .

Great Is His Faithfulness

God has always taken care of me, and my experience on *American Idol* confirmed that truth to me even more. During my last few weeks on the show, I had faith that what was supposed to happen would indeed happen. I was doing all that I could to win, but I wasn't worried that I'd be a failure if I didn't.

I'm so glad that my mom taught me not only how to trust God on those days when I am advancing to the next level of success, but also how to trust Him when things don't work out the way I think they should. Mom taught me that I should always strive to win—and that I should learn how to lose graciously. When we played games at home, Mom refused to simply roll over and let me win. Oh no! If I wanted to win, I'd have to beat her fair and square, and usually I didn't. "It's nice to win," Mom would say, "but it is also important that you learn how to be a gracious loser. So you have to be happy for me that I won."

Consequently, on *American Idol*, while I always gave 150 percent in my efforts to win, I was confident that I could still be happy if someone else won, even if that victory came at my expense.

One Step from the Finale

On the morning of the *American Idol* results show—the show that would determine which two of the three remaining contestants would be in the finale—I was reading an online message by a well-known minister. The message was about how you sometimes can't see right away the reason why certain things happen. You may think the situation should turn out differently, or other people may think it should work out differently. But you have to trust God and trust that He knows what He's doing. The moment I read those words, something struck a chord in my heart. *I think I am going home tonight.* I felt that God was preparing me ahead of time, so I would know that the so-called end of the road was actually a new and exciting path filled with fresh adventures for me.

The night of the Top 3 results show, Ryan Seacrest announced that nearly sixty million votes had been cast after the previous night's show. Jordin Sparks, Blake Lewis, and I held hands as Ryan spoke. First, he called out Jordin, and as Blake and I continued to clutch each other's hands in nervous anticipation, Ryan announced that Jordin had made it through to the finals; she was one of the Top 2. The crowd went crazy and so did I! I was so proud of my baby girl.

"You can have a seat," Ryan said to Jordin after the audience finally calmed down. A hush came over the huge crowd as everyone in the concert hall realized that this was it. One of us—either Blake Lewis or Melinda Doolittle—had been eliminated from the competition.

"Melinda," Ryan called out, "would you step forward?" I let go of Blake's hand and stepped up next to Ryan. When he had called Jordin up, she was safe, but I didn't know if I was safe or if I was gone. I could see Ryan's lips moving and hear him speaking, but his voice seemed to be coming through a giant, slow-motion echo chamber. I stared straight at Ryan as he continued.

"America Has Decided . . ."

"Almost sixty million votes. Again, an incredible number," Ryan said. My lips were tightly pressed together, almost as if I already knew what he was about to say. "Those votes came in," Ryan paused. "America has decided . . ." He paused again and then dropped his voice a bit as he looked at me and said, "that this is the end of the road for you tonight."

I smiled and nodded, and in my peripheral vision, I could see Simon put his hands over his face.

"That means Blake makes it into the *Idol* finale," Ryan continued. "Congratulations, Blake!"

Blake and I hugged, and Jordin's face displayed utter shock. I could feel Ryan turning me around toward the video screen as he said, "Here she is, one of our best singers ever, Melinda Doolittle!"

A video clip of highlights from my performances on the show played on the big screen behind me, but instead of watching, I was thinking. I had a decision to make. Before the last couple of elimination nights, the producers had come up to us and asked what song we would like to sing if we were voted off. Normally, an eliminated contestant sang whatever song he or she had performed the previous night, but the last few weeks had been different because we sang multiple songs on each show. For some reason, I had a hard time deciding what song I wanted to sing, so the producer chose for me, and selected "Nutbush City Limits." However, while my video was playing, I knew I wanted to change that selection. I wanted to sing something that better reflected how I felt at the moment—and I felt empowered! I quickly ran to Ricky Minor and the band and called out, "I want to do 'I'm a Woman!'" I then hurried back to my spot for the end of the video and Ryan's final words.

When the lights came back up, Ryan put his arm around me. "Melinda Doolittle, ladies and gentlemen." Then, as the audience applauded, Ryan said to me, "You've got a lot to do in the future. A lot of great things are going to happen for you."

"Before we say good night," Ryan said, "judges, a quick reaction."

Randy looked up at me from the judges' table. "You've got nothing to be ashamed of. You did the best, you were the most consistent all season, so be proud."

Standing behind the judges' dais, Paula calmly stated,

"You have already made it, Melinda, and now it's time for you to go into your career."

Simon seemed almost sad as he nodded first toward Jordin and Blake. "My congratulations to you two. My commiserations to you, Melinda, because you are one heck of a singer."

Ryan closed out the show by introducing me for the last time as a contestant on *American Idol*. "Right now, she deserves the stage. It is Melinda Doolittle!"

A Smile?

As the band launched into "I'm a Woman," I grabbed the microphone and poured myself into the song. It was my favorite performance yet. While I sang and walked toward the edge of the stage, Blake came out and placed a large bouquet of flowers in Jordin's arms and another in mine. I nodded to him as if to let him know that I was okay with the results. I gave Jordin a wave and pumped my fist in the air as I concluded the song to an explosive round of applause from the wonderfully supportive audience.

When this results show began, I'd had a complete calm and peace in my heart and mind. I knew that, regardless of what happened, it would be okay. When the announcement came that Jordin Sparks and Blake Lewis were the two finalists and I had been voted off the show, I still had perfect peace. My first response was not to burst into tears, but to smile.

For a long time after that, people asked me, “How could you smile when Ryan Seacrest made the announcement?” It was hard to explain to them that I had advance information, really inside information, that didn’t come from Simon, Paula, Randy, or any of the show’s producers. God gave me the peace I needed even before I needed it.

Since I came in third, I supposedly lost the *American Idol* competition. But from my perspective, I didn’t lose; I won! I hadn’t even known what to expect when I first entered the competition, and I surprised myself by getting as far as I did. I hadn’t set out to be a star. Instead, I was conquering my fear of stepping out from being a background singer and into the role of a lead vocalist.

“We’re Good”

When Ryan made the announcement, I recalled my mom’s admonition, “Always lose graciously. Be happy for me that I won.” And I could truthfully say that I was very happy for Jordin and Blake. As for me, my first question was the same one I had asked at every other time of transition: “What’s next? What do You want me to do next, Lord?”

I had asked my mom to come sit in the television studio

audience that week, no small sacrifice since she lived on the East Coast and we taped *Idol* in California. Mom was reticent. "I'm already scheduled to come for the finale a few weeks from now. You're going to be in it, so I can be with you then."

"I know, Mom," I said. "But I think you should come this week, for the Top 3 week."

"Oh, your dad and stepmom and Grandpa and Grandma Doolittle want to go, so I'll let them use this week's tickets. I'll be there in two weeks, though," Mom assured me.

As the music concluded and the television cameras faded to black, marking the end of Top 3 week, Grandpa Doolittle was one of the first people to hug me after Jordin and Blake did. Grandpa Doolittle is a dear man who loves the Lord, and his tremendous faith is combined with straightforward honesty. "Are you upset?" he asked. "Are you sad about this? Should we be sad about this?"

"I'm just fine, Grandpa. I have a perfect peace about it all."

"Well, good. Then we're okay," he said matter-of-factly.

I appreciated Grandpa Doolittle's attitude. He was basically asking, "Are we supposed to cry about this? We'll cry with you if you want us to. Or are you good?"

"I'm good, Grandpa."

"Okay, then we're good."

I could tell that Dad was disappointed that I was not

selected as a finalist. Like any father, he thought his little girl should have won. But after a while, he was also okay with the results. He really had no other alternative.

Grace and Wisdom—and Friendship

It's a good thing that I was okay, because I would have had precious little time to mourn. The next morning we were starting rehearsals for the grand finale, a show on which Jordin, Blake, and I had already been scheduled to perform regardless of who won. Usually after a show in which someone was sent home, the remaining contestants held some sort of farewell party. But because of the extra press demands, Jordin and Blake were whisked away, and I found myself all alone. I had been rooming with Jordin, and since I was no longer a contestant, I had to pack up my things and move out of our room the next day. The contestants who remained in the competition lodged in one of the *American Idol* apartments, but once a person was voted off the show, he or she had to move out. Most people headed back home, but since I was still on the finale, I had to move to a hotel the next day. That night, alone in the apartment before Jordin returned, I reread the online message I had read earlier that day. The words still rang true in my heart and mind. I was convinced that the right thing had happened for Jordin and Blake, and I believed that the right thing had happened for me. I prayed, "Thank You, Lord. I trust You. Give me the grace and wisdom that I need to handle all of this."

Late that night when Jordin returned to our room, she ran to me and hugged me tightly. "I don't understand," she said through her tears. "I really thought you would be in the finale."

"It's okay," I said as I dried her tears. "Now I just need you to go out there and beat Blake."

We laughed loudly, and we talked for a while about what she had to look forward to in the finale and what she might sing. I couldn't have been happier for her. Our friendship had grown immeasurably during our time together on the show.

Mama and Baby Girl

I had met Jordin Sparks during Hollywood Week. During that most stressful week, Jordin's zeal for the competition was infectious. She possessed a joy that simply emanated from her no matter what we were doing or how tired we were. I had never met anyone like her. I knew then, that if we both made it onto the show, we would be fast friends. What I didn't know is what her friendship would mean to me during the competition.

When we arrived in L.A. to begin the live performance phase of the show, Jordin and I clicked immediately. Even with our age difference—she was the youngest on the show, and I was the oldest—I had more in common with her than I did with anyone else. Don't get me wrong, I loved all of the contestants. There is a natural bond that happens when you go through an experience like *American Idol*, and although we were competing against one another, the *Idol* cast and crew quickly became family for me. To this day, when I meet finalists from our season as well as other seasons, we tend to understand one another instantly.

Jordin, however, became my best friend on the show. Because of the age difference, she called me "Mama," and she was my "Baby Girl." Once we made it into the Top 12, *Idol* moved the remaining contestants into apartments, and Jordin and I became roommates. Jordin and her guardian were in one room, and Haley Scarnato and I were in the other. We all hung out together and—I may be biased—we had the most fun apartment. Haley went home during the Top 8 week, so Jordin and I were left in the apartment. We would stay up and talk, go over our songs together, and pray for each other, and we vowed to be a rock for the other for our entire time on the show. Little did we know, we would be there together for the entire season.

What I most admire about Jordin is her undying faith. She is a firm believer that God knows what He's doing and that He has a purpose and a plan for all of us. It was so reassuring to hear those words from her during my stay on *American Idol*. There were many times when we would get nervous right before walking out on stage, so Jordin and I always stopped right then and said a prayer together. I don't know if there will ever be a way to describe how much that meant to me or how those prayers helped me through the show. To this day, Jordin still calls me "Mama," and I don't think there's a way I could ever be more proud of my "Baby Girl" than I am. Jordin's kindness and compassion toward me the night I was voted off *Idol* will be forever imbedded in my heart and mind. She has remained a wonderful friend to me and has been a godsend in my life.

Hardly a Loser!

Early the next morning, a production assistant from the show met me at the apartment and drove me to a hotel, where I checked in. Then I got back in the car to return to rehearsals for the *American Idol* finale.

Sometimes people still try to console me by saying, "Oh, I'm so sorry that you lost." Although I don't usually say it, I sometimes want to yell, *I didn't lose; I won!* I understand the hierarchy of awards, that I came in third place rather than first. I get that. But I didn't lose. Coming in third was a major achievement for me. Moreover, my appearance on *American Idol* catapulted my career to increasingly higher levels.

Beyond that, I have been thrilled at what God did through me on *American Idol*. While we contestants were singing all sorts of songs made popular by artists such as Bon Jovi, Diana Ross, Barry Gibb, and others, somehow, something about me connected with the audience. In truth, the impact was beyond me, far beyond anything I could have produced on my own. People said a light seemed to shine through me, a light that brought some people out of the shadows, a light that brightened the dark places in some people's lives, and a light that further illuminated the path for those already enjoying the sunshine. If nothing else ever came of my *American Idol* experience, that connection with the audience alone would have been enough to make me feel like I won. But so much more has developed. Because of being on the show, I get to do something that I've discovered I really love: I can share a message of hope! I get to encourage and affect people positively simply by being me!

12

Beyond Me

An interviewer asked me, "Melinda, if you could have anything you wanted and cost was not a factor, what would you want?"

After thinking about it for a moment, I replied, "I want a bigger voice to make a difference. Not a louder voice, but a bigger one, a larger platform from which I can encourage others." That's what my life is all about. I want to be in a place where I can help others realize their dreams.

From the day I discovered that I wanted to sing, when that Whitney Houston song came on in the store and I watched people stop and listen, I knew I wanted my music to stop people, grab their attention, and then pull them into something good.

To me, success is being able to do what you love, to love what you do, and to make a living at it. I get to wake up every day and sing! Better yet, I have the opportunity to make a difference in the lives of children through various organizations such as The LEAGUE and Malaria No More. I enjoy working with young children who are so impressionable, and I hope I show them a deep, genuine love in the process. I tell kids, "You don't have to be on TV to make a difference. You just have to be you!"

Set Some New Goals

I look at setting goals as establishing a faith wall, and setting goals will be, for me, a lifelong process of finding new milestones that I want to achieve and keeping them in front of me so I can be reminded of them regularly. Certainly, our goals change as we go through life. At one point, for instance, I planned to be a background singer for a mainstream artist in order to reach a mainstream audience and hopefully bring some light and joy to people who may never set foot in a church. Now, I am that artist.

Something Greater at Work

When I was young, I responded to every invitation to ask Jesus into my heart. Oh, at five years of age, I didn't have a bunch to repent over, but I was determined to do it, so my mom didn't discourage me. I had heard a number of messages about "inviting Jesus to live in your heart," and I pictured my relationship with the Lord just that way. I thought He had a tiny, little house within my heart, and that's where He lived. Whenever I did anything wrong, I was certain that I had offended Him and that He had moved out. So at every altar call I heard, upon every "invitation to meet Jesus" that I heard, I responded and asked Jesus to come back into my heart. I was so glad when I realized that He had never really left—even if I had done something that displeased Him.

Somewhere around my eighth birthday, I made a commitment to live in a way that I would try to do the right thing. Since then, my spiritual life has been a fascinating journey. I don't feel that I have arrived, but I'm enjoying the trip.

I get up each day and say something like, "I trust You today. And if something doesn't go the way I think it should, that's okay, because I know You are looking out for me." Each new day is a fresh adventure.

Every singer or musician who has ever stood in front of an audience knows the feeling—when it seems that everything about the show is working. The sound is perfect, the lights are creating just the right ambiance, and the crowd "gets" what you are trying to put out there—every true artist knows deep within that overwhelming sense that something more is happening than mere music. Something greater, something bigger, is at work. That's how I feel when I step up to use the gift God has given to me.

I am still in awe at what God has done in my life. In fact, I am amazed by God, period. What He does for, in, and through me is far . . . far . . . beyond me.

Share Your Thoughts

With the Author: Your comments will be forwarded to the author when you send them to *zauthor@zondervan.com*.

With Zondervan: Submit your review of this book by writing to *zreview@zondervan.com*.

Free Online Resources at

www.zondervan.com

Zondervan AuthorTracker: Be notified whenever your favorite authors publish new books, go on tour, or post an update about what's happening in their lives at www.zondervan.com/authortracker.

Daily Bible Verses and Devotions: Enrich your life with daily Bible verses or devotions that help you start every morning focused on God. Visit www.zondervan.com/newsletters.

Free Email Publications: Sign up for newsletters on Christian living, academic resources, church ministry, fiction, children's resources, and more. Visit www.zondervan.com/newsletters.

Zondervan Bible Search: Find and compare Bible passages in a variety of translations at www.zondervanbiblesearch.com.

Other Benefits: Register yourself to receive online benefits like coupons and special offers, or to participate in research.

ZONDERVAN®

ZONDERVAN.com/
AUTHORTRACKER
follow your favorite authors